A Bird in the Hand

A Comedy

Derek Benfield

Samuel French - London
New York – Sydney – Toronto – Hollywood

Copyright © 1973 by Derek Benfield
All Rights Reserved

A BIRD IN THE HAND is fully protected under the copyright laws of the British Commonwealth, including Canada, the United States of America, and all other countries of the Copyright Union. All rights, including professional and amateur stage productions, recitation, lecturing, public reading, motion picture, radio broadcasting, television and the rights of translation into foreign languages are strictly reserved.

ISBN 978-0-573-11508-0

www.samuelfrench.co.uk
www.samuelfrench.com

FOR AMATEUR PRODUCTION ENQUIRIES

UNITED KINGDOM AND WORLD
EXCLUDING NORTH AMERICA
plays@samuelfrench.co.uk
020 7255 4302/01

Each title is subject to availability from Samuel French, depending upon country of performance.

CAUTION: Professional and amateur producers are hereby warned that A BIRD IN THE HAND is subject to a licensing fee. Publication of this play does not imply availability for performance. Both amateurs and professionals considering a production are strongly advised to apply to the appropriate agent before starting rehearsals, advertising, or booking a theatre. A licensing fee must be paid whether the title is presented for charity or gain and whether or not admission is charged.

The professional rights in this play are controlled by Samuel French Ltd, 24-32 Stephenson Way, London, NW1 2HD.

No one shall make any changes in this title for the purpose of production. No part of this book may be reproduced, stored in a retrieval system, or transmitted in any form, by any means, now known or yet to be invented, including mechanical, electronic, photocopying, recording, videotaping, or otherwise, without the prior written permission of the publisher. No one shall upload this title, or part of this title, to any social media websites.

The right of Derek Benfield to be identified as author of this work has been asserted in accordance with Section 77 of the Copyright, Designs and Patents Act 1988.

CHARACTERS

SYLVIA WINTON

MAX WINTON

MISS FERGUSON

PERCH

HARRY TYLER

PEGGY

SUE

GEORGE STEVENS

HELEN

FRANCES

The play takes place in Max Winton's flat in a fashionable part of London.

ACT ONE   An Autumn evening.

ACT TWO   An hour later.

ACT THREE   The following evening.

PRODUCTION NOTE

'A Bird in the Hand' is a comedy about marriage, about attitudes and relationships; but mainly about two men who have completely divergent views on the subject of matrimony. It is also about men who have reached the dreaded 40's but whose feelings and emotions are still firmly planted in the past and who are reluctant to accept the inevitable advance of time.

Max and Harry are old friends who in their younger days shared a common lust for life and a love of booze and women. Their friendship will continue to last in spite of the stresses that occasionally are put upon it. Their gay bachelordom ended abruptly when both took the inevitable step to the altar. Max married Sylvia and they have remained together for twelve years. Harry, however, has tried and failed three times and is now a confirmed bachelor once more, having learned his lesson the hard way. When he learns, therefore, that Max's apparently stable marriage has at last foundered and that Sylvia has packed and gone, he receives the news with great delight. He imagines that he and Max can now resume their old status and pick up the threads of their lost life of gaiety and girls. He packs his toothbrush, orders some drink, looks out the 'little red book' of telephone numbers and comes round to celebrate - only to find that after twenty-four hours Sylvia is back home again, not to cement the marriage but with a slightly more permissive view of things.

Max and Harry, with varying degrees of enthusiasm, attempt to set up their old bachelor pad once more and to recapture the good life. But it isn't made easy with Sylvia constantly in and out, aiding and abetting their efforts and only succeeding in sabotaging them. Finally they are forced to bow to the inevitable. Harry, the eternal optimist, determines to stay in the hunt, though necessarily lowering his sights a degree or two; while Max, after a brave effort, decides that the old days have lost their appeal and that a bird in the hand like Sylvia is definitely preferable to all the dollies hanging from the trees.

This is a comedy, and its riotous moments must never go over the border into farce. The relationships are real. The dilemma between Max and Sylvia over her career, for example, is a very serious one. Max is an appealing, somewhat pathetic person in sharp contrast to the more ebullient self-confidence of Harry. Sylvia is warm-hearted, smooth, sophisticated and well-dressed. A career woman, yes, but never brittle. We must always want their marriage to succeed.

There are a number of quite sentimental moments in the play which serve to heighten the comedy, so don't shy away from them. For example, Helen and Frances are not eccentric characters. They are funny, yes, but they are also sad, and the scene between Harry and Max after they have left (page 106) should be quite moving. The relationship between Frances and Max, too, is full of poignant memory. They had rapport in the old days and they still have.

Greta is about thirty, a studious intelligent girl. Plain, obviously not the catch of the season, but she is a pleasant enough girl and should not be permanently falling over the furniture! Perch will present no problems to the good character actor. He admires and envies Harry and Max in their various subterfuges and intrigues and can scarcely conceal his enjoyment. Stevens is fussy and pompous, quick of movement and looks even younger than his thirty-seven years, while Peggy and Sue are all they seem to be - a couple of dolly birds with their hearts (and everything else) in the right place.

Make the setting as sumptuous as possible. It is a luxury pad overlooking Hyde Park and it is Autumn, so go to town on the décor and lighting.

I did not write 'A Bird in the Hand' to put over any profound truths or to make a personal comment on the married state. I wrote it simply to entertain. I hope you will think that I have succeeded.

                                                            Derek Benfield

A BIRD IN THE HAND

ACT ONE

MAX WINTON's comfortably furnished London flat on the second floor of a fashionable block overlooking the park. The main door from the hall is U.L., and as you come in you descend two steps into the living-room. A large window occupies most of the back wall U.R., with a padded window seat below it. The door D.R. leads to the rest of the flat. There is a recess in the wall U.L. where the record player and various L.P.s live, with bookshelves above and a cupboard beneath. There is a table D.L. with drinks. A large comfortable sofa is set at an angle L.C., with a table behind it and a wastepaper basket L. of it. A big leather armchair is R.C. and a small tub chair in front of the table D.L. The telephone is on the sofa table. The main light switch is by the door U.L. and there are various lamps that operate individually. Throughout the play, L. and R. refer to the actors' L. and R.

It is an autumn evening. As the curtain rises, SYLVIA WINTON is bursting through the door from the hall, weighed down with parcels, cases, etc. She is a very attractive woman of about 40. She sails in serenely to C., followed by MAX WINTON. He is 43, in shirt sleeves and a small, dainty apron, and in a high state of distress.

MAX	What do you think you're doing?
SYLVIA	Coming back, of course.
MAX	You can't do that!
SYLVIA	Why not? I live here.
MAX	Not any more. You abdicated that right the moment you walked out of that door with your bags packed.
SYLVIA	(serenely) Well, now I'm walking back in again and unpacking them. (She puts down her cases L. of the armchair.)
MAX	You can't!
SYLVIA	Don't keep saying 'You can't'. I just have.
MAX	But that's immoral!
SYLVIA	Living with my own husband?
MAX	You aren't. I mean - I'm not. Not any more.
SYLVIA	Oh, yes, you are. I bet you haven't even filled in the forms yet.
MAX	I've hardly had the time! You've only been gone twenty-four hours! You said you'd never see me again.
SYLVIA	I know.
MAX	Well, then?
SYLVIA	That was yesterday.
	(She puts down her parcels on the armchair. He follows her in a dither.)
MAX	What changed your mind?
SYLVIA	I felt sorry for you.
MAX	I don't need your pity.
SYLVIA	I suddenly thought of you, trying to cope all on your own. You never were very good at coping, were you? Just look at that dear little apron!
	(He tears off the apron and dashes it down, moving below the sofa.)

A BIRD IN THE HAND

              Why didn't you go out to eat like you usually do?

MAX   I wanted a change.

SYLVIA   Cooking an omelette?

MAX   No!

SYLVIA   What, then?

MAX   Never you mind.

SYLVIA   Oh, come on - tell me.

MAX   Well, if you must know - frozen kipper fillets.

             (She laughs.)

             And there's no need to laugh. I happen to like them.

SYLVIA   You used not to.   (Picks up her cases.)

MAX   How would you know? You never used to care what I was eating. You were always far too busy in your office!

SYLVIA   Oh, now don't start that again, darling.

MAX   What?

SYLVIA   (crossing with cases to D.R.)   All that stuff about woman's place being in the home. It's terribly old-fashioned, you know.   (Puts down her cases.)

MAX   (moving D.C.)   I just happen to think that a man shouldn't have to stand in line behind his wife's career. Do you know - sometimes you weren't in for dinner for three whole weeks? The waiter at the Chinese restaurant began to wonder why I didn't move my bed in there!

SYLVIA   You always said you liked Chinese food.

MAX   After three weeks even my breakfast egg was tasting sweet and sour.

SYLVIA   (moving to her parcels)   If you wanted to eat in all the time you should have married a cook.

MAX   Sylvia - you know it wasn't just the dinner. I - I just wanted to see you occasionally.

             (There is a pause as they look at each other.)

SYLVIA	Like I wanted to see you when we were first married? Remember those nights?	
MAX	You know that was different.	
SYLVIA	(gently sarcastic) Oh, yes - of course! You're a man. I was forgetting.	
MAX	I was working for that damn film company in those days! I spent half my nights hanging about airport lounges waiting for so-called V.I.P.'s. Didn't you know that all the time I was wanting to be with you?	
SYLVIA	All I knew was that I was alone. Why do you think I took this job in the first place? If I wasn't able to have children and I couldn't have you, I was at least going to have a life that belonged to me.	
MAX	It's - it's different now.	
SYLVIA	You bet it's different. I've got this job now - I'm a bloody good journalist. And what is more, I enjoy it. You can't expect me to give it all up.	
MAX	(turning away from her) Is that all you came back for? To pick up the fight where we left off?	
SYLVIA	No.	
MAX	(turning to look at her) What, then?	
SYLVIA	Oh, I - I got thinking. You're right, of course, about a lot of things. I neglected you dreadfully. But - now it's all going to be different.	
MAX	(moving a pace towards her) You are giving up your job, then?	
SYLVIA	No, but I -	
MAX	Then don't start putting everything down all over the place - (He starts collecting up her various parcels and handing them back to her.) - because you're not staying!	
SYLVIA	(ignoring this and crossing with the shopping bag to D.L.) I've brought some steak and a bottle of wine for dinner.	
MAX	Thank you, but I've already done my cooking. (He still has her parcels in his arms.)	

A BIRD IN THE HAND

SYLVIA	Sirloin. (She puts the bottle of wine on the table D.L.)
MAX	What?
SYLVIA	With button mushrooms and French salad.
MAX	I'm sticking to my kippers.
SYLVIA	By now they'll be sticking to the pan.
MAX	(the martyr) I'll manage. So please take these and go away. (GRETA FERGUSON comes in, tentatively. She is a somewhat studious girl of about 30, wearing glasses and carrying a portable typewriter. She comes to above the sofa.) Who the hell's this?
SYLVIA	You remember Greta.
MAX	No, I do not remember Greta. I've never seen her before in my life! (SYLVIA moves to L. of sofa.)
SYLVIA	(to GRETA) Don't take any notice of him. He's all upset because I ruined his kipper fillets. He'll simmer down presently. Did you manage to park the car?
GRETA	Round the corner. (Puts her handbag on R. end of sofa.)
SYLVIA	Oh, good. (To MAX.) Miss Ferguson is my secretary.
GRETA	And this is my typewriter. (She holds up her typewriter, moving to U.R. of the sofa.)
MAX	(L. of the armchair) How do you do.
GRETA	It's a Remington.
MAX	Couldn't you bear to be parted from it?
SYLVIA	She'd be no good without it, would she?
MAX	(eyeing GRETA without enthusiasm) I believe you.
SYLVIA	So she brought it with her. (She returns to the table D.L. and checks the food in the shopping bag.)

MAX	What for?	
SYLVIA	(casually) To type letters for me, of course.	

(MAX crosses to below the sofa.)

MAX	Here?
SYLVIA	Yes.
MAX	Sylvia, you seem to be forgetting - you don't live here any more.

(GRETA giggles, and he turns to her. She reacts and moves away to below the armchair.)

Anyhow, sometimes I have work to do at home. You're not coming in and out of here - tapping away on that thing. How could I concentrate?

GRETA	I won't disturb you.
MAX	No, you won't! (He turns to SYLVIA.) They can't come in here - either of them.
SYLVIA	(to him, reasonably) But, darling, she's my secretary.
GRETA	And this is my typewriter. (She holds it up again.)
MAX	Then they should both be in the office - covered over in black until you need them in the morning.
SYLVIA	But I shall be here in the morning.
MAX	What?
SYLVIA	You were always complaining about the time I spent at the office, so in future I'm going to do more work from home. (She takes the parcels from him.)
MAX	But there is no future - we are getting divorced.
SYLVIA	Yes, I know that. But, in the meantime, somebody's got to look after you, haven't they?

(SYLVIA crosses below MAX to the door D.R.)

Come along, Greta. I'll show you where you'll be sleeping.

MAX	(to D.C.) She won't be sleeping here. And neither will you.

SYLVIA	What are you going to do, then? Call Perch and have us evicted? I'm putting her in the back room, next to mine.
MAX	She's not sleeping here!
SYLVIA	Of course she is, darling. After all, now that you and I are separated, you could hardly expect me to live under the same roof without a chaperone. (She and GRETA go off R., all smiles.)

(MAX moves to D.R.C. and gazes after them.)

MAX	(calling) Chaperone? That's the last thing you'll need!

(PERCH, the liftman, comes in with a large crate of drink. He is a north countryman of about 50, with the air of an old soldier.)

PERCH	Where will you 'ave it, sir?
MAX	What?
PERCH	The booze.
MAX	I didn't order any booze.
PERCH	(to L. of sofa) No, sir - Mr. Tyler did. Rang me this afternoon.
MAX	(to below sofa) And told you to deliver it here?
PERCH	Yes, sir.
MAX	He was quick off the mark.
PERCH	He said to prepare for a party.
MAX	Well, it looks as if you've done that all right. I suppose you'd better put it over there, Perch.

(PERCH takes the drinks to the table D.L.)

PERCH	Bloke in the off-licence asked if I was getting ready for prohibition.
MAX	I'm not surprised.

(PERCH moves to MAX.)

PERCH	Makes a change from two brown ales and a packet of crisps, I can tell you. Still, it isn't every day, is it?

8   A BIRD IN THE HAND   Act 1

MAX   What isn't?

PERCH The day of freedom! Something to celebrate. I wish I could be rid of my missus so easily. Reckon you were born lucky, sir.

MAX   Oh - yes - rather.   (He casts a nervous glance R.)

PERCH But at least you were firm - put your foot down. I admire that in a man, sir. Master in your own house - 'Out you go' - and out she went.

MAX   Yes. Yes, she did do that, didn't she?

PERCH I think there's plenty there, sir.

MAX   Yes - right - thank you, Perch.

(As PERCH prepares to leave, SYLVIA returns and crosses to the armchair for the last parcel.)

SYLVIA Hullo, Perch.

(He turns and sees her.)

PERCH Oh, my God!

SYLVIA You don't sound very pleased to see me.

PERCH Beg your pardon, madam. Delighted, of course. Bit of a surprise, you might say. Nice to see you back, madam. (He turns to MAX as he goes to the door.)   Didn't last long, did it, sir?

MAX   What?

PERCH The revolution!   (He goes out L.)

SYLVIA Dear old Perch. He hasn't changed a bit.

MAX   (surly)   What did you expect? You've only been gone one day.

(SYLVIA sees the drinks and crosses to get a closer look.)

SYLVIA Whatever's all this?

MAX   Oh - er - just a few bottles.

SYLVIA Darling, you are sweet!   (She embraces him.)

MAX   What are you talking about?

A BIRD IN THE HAND 9

SYLVIA   You knew all the time, didn't you?

MAX   Knew what?

SYLVIA   That I'd be coming back.

MAX   No, I didn't! As a matter of fact - I didn't order those drinks. Harry did.

SYLVIA   Harry?

MAX   Yes.

SYLVIA   (below him to D.C.)   I might have guessed. You told him about us, then?

MAX   Er - yes. He rang last night.

SYLVIA   I bet he was delighted. After all, he knows all about broken marriages. He must have been so glad to know that yours had failed as well.

MAX   (to her)   As a matter of fact, he was very upset.

         (She turns.)

SYLVIA   Not too upset to order the booze for the celebration, though.

MAX   Sylvia - nobody's celebrating.

SYLVIA   Commiserating, then. Call it what you like. It's still a lot of booze. Looks as if you were laying in for a siege. Couldn't you have waited twenty-four hours?

MAX   How did I know you were coming back? I thought the flat would be empty. I thought I'd be alone - and, as a matter of fact, I didn't want to be alone!

         (A pause. They look at each other.)

SYLVIA   You're still in love with me.

MAX   No, I'm not.

SYLVIA   I bet you are.   (She advances on him.)

MAX   (backing)   I'll call Miss Ferguson.

SYLVIA   Call who you like. I think I'm going to kiss you.

MAX   I shall struggle.

SYLVIA   I'm stronger than you are.

MAX		You don't have to tell me. I've got the marks to prove it. If you come any nearer, I'll scream.
SYLVIA		(with a smile) You know, I really think you would. (With sudden suspicion.) Have you and Harry got some girls coming in tonight?
MAX		Girls?
SYLVIA		You know what girls are.
MAX		What do you take me for?
SYLVIA		Oh, come on, now -
MAX		(on the defensive) If we had, you would be in no position to complain.
SYLVIA		I'm not complaining. I'm asking.
MAX		Your face is complaining. (Circling above the sofa to U.C.) Remember, it was you who finally decided to walk out on me -
SYLVIA		(following him) You were pushing pretty hard -
MAX		And the moment you did that, you let go of the reins and I was free to gallop wherever I liked.
SYLVIA		I hardly expected you to gallop over to the nearest bunch of loose mares the minute I was out of sight!
MAX		But I didn't! Look, it was you who started talking about girls.
SYLVIA		All right, then - how many?
MAX		What?
SYLVIA		Girls!

(A pause. MAX sits in the armchair, sorry for himself.)

MAX		None.
SYLVIA		None?
MAX		(quietly) I spoke to Harry. He said he'd come over tonight. We were going to have a quiet evening - you know - two old friends consoling one another - have a few beers - maybe watch the football on the television.

A BIRD IN THE HAND 11

SYLVIA   No party?

MAX   No.

SYLVIA   No girls?

MAX   No.

SYLVIA   All that drink just for you and Harry?

MAX   Yes!

SYLVIA   Well, you ought to be ashamed of yourselves!   (She goes out R.)

(The doorbell rings.)

MAX   Oh, my God!

(He goes out to the front door. A few seconds later HARRY TYLER comes in, briskly. HARRY is a little older than MAX, assured and self-confident, an attractive personality, but with the slightly crusty exterior of the man who has been through the mill. He swoops in, puts down his hat and briefcase on the sofa table and moves C. MAX follows him and they meet below the sofa. HARRY beams enthusiastically.)

HARRY   Max!   (He takes him by the shoulders.)   Welcome to the club! You look better already. Quite a new man. And this is only after twenty-four hours. Think what a couple of months'll do for you. We'll soon get rid of that healthy look.

MAX   Harry, as a matter of fact -

HARRY   Please! Don't start regretting. You took the right step. Believe me, I know. Of course it feels strange at first - but never regret. Never look back. You're on the threshold of a new world! The booze arrive okay?

MAX   Over there.

HARRY   (crossing to it)   Oh - great.

MAX   You didn't have to do that, you know. I had a couple of bottles in.

HARRY   They'll do for starters.

MAX	(taking a pace towards him) But, Harry, there's something I haven't -	
HARRY	If you're going to start weeping on my shoulder, I'm going right out again. Positive thinking. That's what we've got to have. Positive thinking.	
MAX	Yes. I suppose so - (He wanders uncomfortably to above the sofa.)	
HARRY	Max - we are going to have a ball! (He picks up a bottle of Scotch.) Just look at that. H'm - (He kisses the bottle.) - there isn't a lovelier sight. I may not be sober for the rest of the month.	

(MAX has picked up the briefcase HARRY has brought in.)

MAX	What's in here?
HARRY	What do you think? Pyjamas and toothbrush. I always carry spares.
MAX	You can't stay here.
HARRY	Don't worry. I won't cramp your style. Believe me, when the time comes, I'll be invisible. (He sits, relaxed, L. end of the sofa.)
MAX	(round to L. of the sofa) But, Harry, you don't understand -

(The door R. opens and GRETA comes in. HARRY reacts and watches her as she walks across without looking at them, picks up her handbag and goes straight out again. HARRY looks at MAX disdainfully.)

HARRY	What was that?
MAX	Er - the girl?
HARRY	Is that what it was?
MAX	(below sofa to C.) She - er she comes here every day.
HARRY	Oh, Max - her? You disappoint me.
MAX	No, no! She's the - er - the daily lady.
HARRY	Daily lady?

A BIRD IN THE HAND

MAX   Yes.

HARRY   What's she doing here at night?

MAX   She was late starting.

HARRY   Looking at her, it's a wonder she started at all.

MAX   (to below R. end of sofa)   Oh, she's a very good worker!

HARRY   She'd need to be.   (Suspiciously.)   Now, look here, Max - what do you want with a daily lady like that?

MAX   Oh, it's not what you think.

HARRY   Well, that's a relief. I thought for a moment you'd opened the door and let in the first stray that came around.

MAX   Miss Ferguson? Good lord, no!

HARRY   I should hope not. You're now a free man. You can afford to be choosy.

(MAX sits beside HARRY.)

MAX   I can?

HARRY   You're now rid of the shackles. It's worth ten years off your life - you see. You are now a marketable commodity.

MAX   Harry, for God's sake! You make me sound like a melon.

HARRY   Have you been married so long you've forgotten what it's like?

MAX   What what's like?

HARRY   Oh, my God! You really have forgotten. We're going to have to work on that memory of yours. Never mind. I have spread the word.

MAX   What word?

HARRY   Max - is - a - free - man. I tell you, every available bird within fifty miles will soon be heading this way.

MAX   Wh - What for?

(HARRY looks at him, unbelievingly.)

HARRY   Max, have you forgotten the old days? You and me - and all those girls. Have you forgotten the times we used to have?

MAX   We certainly lived a little.

HARRY   Lived a little? We invented it!

MAX   Well, even if we didn't, we behaved as if we did.

HARRY   Do you remember that blonde girl - what was her name - Pinky Blantyre!

MAX   What a memory!

HARRY   She really was something. A big girl with a big punch. Nearly broke my back.

MAX   She knocked you down?

HARRY   No. I fell off the bed. Took me all my time to get up again. And how about the Hessler twins? Remember? They were great. Two for the price of one.

MAX   (dreamily)   Yes - they were sweet girls, all right.

HARRY   You know something I never found out? Which one did you get?

(They laugh, enjoying the memories.)

You see - you do remember. There was the old look in your eye then. There is still hope. The patient may yet survive. Don't you see, Max - it'll be those days all over again. I may even move in here. Shack up with you, and all we'll have to do is go through the little books and lift the phone! What do you say?

MAX   That was all a long time ago.

HARRY   Max, they don't do it any different now! The rules may be altered but the game hasn't changed.

MAX   It - it wouldn't work, Harry.

HARRY   What d'you mean it wouldn't work?

MAX   We're older now.

HARRY   You speak for yourself.

A BIRD IN THE HAND

MAX   I'm forty-three! So what does that make you?

HARRY   Never you mind what that makes me!   (Pause.) Anyhow, what's the matter with thirty-nine?

MAX   (laughing)   Thirty-nine?

HARRY   Don't say it like that.

MAX   You haven't been thirty-nine for six years.

HARRY   Oh, yes, I have! And I intend being thirty-nine for another six. Anyhow, who cares about middle-age? Girls prefer older men.

MAX   That's what the older men say.

HARRY   Max, what is the matter with you?

MAX   I'm only being realistic.

HARRY   No, you're not. You're being pessimistic. And, what is more, you're depressing me. I'll have to have a drink. (He rises and goes to help himself.)

MAX   After all, why should all these birds you talk about come flocking here because of me? Over forty and only just unmarried.

HARRY   Don't undersell yourself, Max. You're a successful man.

MAX   I wish you'd tell my bank manager that.

HARRY   Oh, come on, now - you're a highly paid advertising executive. You must earn more than I do.

     (SYLVIA comes in. HARRY reacts. MAX rises to R. of the sofa.)

SYLVIA   Hullo, Harry.   (To below the armchair.)

HARRY   Oh, my God!

SYLVIA   You're the second person who's said that to me in ten minutes.

HARRY   (crossing to her)   What are you doing here?

SYLVIA   Sorry to disappoint you, Harry, but I came back.

HARRY   (turning to MAX)   Max - ?

MAX	That's what she did all right.	
HARRY	You knew she was there all the time?	
MAX	Er - yes.	
HARRY	(with sudden realisation) Oh, I get it! You mean you forgot something, you came back to get it and now you're leaving?	
SYLVIA	I forgot something all right.	
HARRY	(relaxing) That's okay, then. You had me worried for a minute. You came in that door like a fixture. Well, why don't we give you a hand, eh? Come on, Max. Whatever it was Sylvia forgot we can find it for her and send her on her way.	
MAX	You'll never guess what it was she forgot.	
HARRY	(aside to MAX) Never mind the party games! Let's just get her out of here.	
SYLVIA	I forgot him.	
HARRY	What? (He turns to MAX.)	
MAX	(weakly) That's right.	
SYLVIA	So - I came back.	
HARRY	But I thought that was the idea - that you were to forget him. Forget each other - that was what it was all about! You didn't have to come back.	
SYLVIA	It was a good thing I did. Do you know what he was cooking for his dinner?	
HARRY	Frozen kipper fillets?	
SYLVIA	How did you know?	
HARRY	Because that's what I started on! It's what all we new bachelors start on. But it's not the end of the world. You work your way up from there! I'll have to have another drink. (He goes to help himself.)	
SYLVIA	You didn't waste any time ordering the booze, did you, Harry? News certainly travels fast around here.	

A BIRD IN THE HAND

HARRY You want a drink?

SYLVIA No, thank you. I don't need it.   (She sits in the armchair.)

HARRY Very funny. So that was why you came back, eh, Sylvia? After all these years you were suddenly concerned about what he was going to have for his dinner.

SYLVIA Nothing wrong in that, is there?

HARRY No. Just surprising, that's all. You could have sent him a cookery book.

MAX (laughing nervously)   I told her I could manage.

HARRY Well - glad to hear from you, Max! I thought you were holding your breath or something.   (He moves to him.)   What happened to the positive action? You stand up for your rights - throw your wife out - and in twenty-four hours she's coming back to you.

MAX I didn't ask her to! She just walked in.

SYLVIA (smiling)   I still had my latchkey.

HARRY You mean to say you didn't ask her for the key?

MAX Well, neither did you when your wife left!

HARRY No - but the moment she'd gone I had the lock changed.

SYLVIA Anyway, I'm not.

HARRY Not what?

SYLVIA Coming back to him.

HARRY You just did.

SYLVIA Yes, but we're still going to be divorced.

(HARRY, bemused, looks from SYLVIA to MAX, finishes his drink quickly and goes to replenish his glass.)

Perhaps you'd like a bigger glass?

HARRY You're - you're still going to be divorced?

SYLVIA That's what Max wants. Isn't it, darling?

MAX Yes - that's right!

18   A BIRD IN THE HAND   Act 1

HARRY   So what are you doing here?
SYLVIA   Looking after him.
HARRY   Until you get divorced?
SYLVIA   Yes.
HARRY   That'll give the judge a laugh.

            (MISS FERGUSON comes in. SYLVIA goes to meet her D.R.C.)

SYLVIA   Ah, Greta! Come and meet Harry.
HARRY   (bluntly)   We've already met.   (To GRETA.) Isn't it time you went home?
SYLVIA   Don't take any notice of him. He's an old man and he's forgotten his manners.
HARRY   (to below L. end of the sofa)   Max, pay her off and let her go, eh?
SYLVIA   Pay her?
HARRY   I've never known a daily lady hang around so long.
SYLVIA   (icily)   Miss Ferguson happens to be my secretary.

            (HARRY looks at MAX, coldly.)

HARRY   Thank you, Max. I'll do the same for you sometime.
MAX   I - I don't know what made me say it. Sort of a joke, I suppose.
HARRY   Not a very good sort of joke.
MAX   As a matter of fact - she's staying here.
HARRY   Miss Ferguson?

            (GRETA goes to HARRY.)

GRETA   How do you do.
HARRY   Not as well as I thought.   (To MAX.)   She's staying here, as well?
MAX   Yes.
HARRY   What is this? The Y.W.C.A.?   (Diplomatically.)

A BIRD IN THE HAND

	Look, Sylvia - there's no need for you and Miss Ferguson to stay around. I've already fixed up dinner for Max to-night.
SYLVIA	Yes. I bet you have! I bet you've had it organised ever since we got back from the honeymoon.
GRETA	(to SYLVIA) Is he trying to get rid of us?
SYLVIA	You know - I get the same feeling. What time are the others coming, Harry?
MAX	I told you -
HARRY	(glancing at his watch) They'll be here in twenty minutes.
	(MAX looks surprised.)
MAX	What?
SYLVIA	Oh - so it's not going to be a quiet sort of evening with two old friends consoling one another.
	(MAX shrinks as she ends up looking at him.)
	I had a feeling all that drink was too much - even for two old friends.
HARRY	(innocently) Have I said something?
MAX	Yes - you said something.
HARRY	So I invited some of the boys in. What's wrong with that? This was supposed to be a celebration.
SYLVIA	Well - until the boys arrive - I expect you'd like a little feminine company. (Sits R. end of sofa.)
MAX	Sylvia, believe me, I had no idea -
SYLVIA	So Greta and I may as well have a little drink. Sit down, Greta.
	(She does so in the chair D.L.)
	Vodka for me, please, Harry.
	(HARRY, for a second off-balance, goes obediently to the drinks table.)
	(to GRETA) What'll you have?

GRETA	Coca-cola, please.	
HARRY	(bluntly)	We haven't got any.
GRETA	I'll have vodka, then.	

(The men react.)

I prefer coke, though.

HARRY Yes, so do I, but I'm going on a cure.

SYLVIA You'll help yourself, won't you, Harry? Like you always do.

HARRY Same old Sylvia.

SYLVIA (to MAX, who is looking disconsolate) Do cheer up, darling. Come and sit down next to me. After all, this was supposed to be a celebration.

(MAX obediently goes and sits on her L.)

(HARRY brings the drinks to them.)

GRETA Thanks.

SYLVIA Thank you, Harry.

(HARRY sits down slightly away from them in the armchair R.C. There is quite a pause.)

Well - what shall we drink to?

HARRY It was going to be 'Absent friends'.

GRETA (suddenly) I've brought my typewriter!

HARRY Well, we can't drink to that.

(PERCH comes in with a carrier bag containing food. He brings it to R. of the sofa.)

PERCH I've got it 'ere, madam.

MAX What have you got there?

PERCH (with a guilty look at SYLVIA) Er - the food, sir. Mrs Winton asked me -

SYLVIA Yes. You see, I only brought enough for three, so I rang through from the bedroom. When I knew Harry was coming, I guessed he wouldn't be coming alone. You don't mind, do you?

A BIRD IN THE HAND

MAX	(to PERCH) Whose side are you on?
PERCH	I thought the war was over, sir.
MAX	Well, you thought wrong.
PERCH	Just a temporary truce?
MAX	You take your orders from me.
PERCH	Yes, sir. Sorry, sir.
SYLVIA	Put it in the kitchen, please, Perch.
	(PERCH hesitates, looks at MAX.)
MAX	Er - put it in the kitchen, will you?
PERCH	Thank you, sir. (He pauses near HARRY as he passes, and speaks confidentially.) Not exactly what we expected, eh, sir? Total collapse on all fronts.
HARRY	Don't worry. There's bound to be a counter-offensive.
PERCH	I hope so. All I can say, sir, is thank God for your example.
HARRY	Thank you, Perch.
	(PERCH goes out D.R. with the food.)
SYLVIA	What was that all about?
HARRY	He was asking the way to the kitchen.
GRETA	Are you married, Mr Tyler?
HARRY	Not any more. I did it once and didn't like it.
SYLVIA	Once? You did it three times.
GRETA	Three times?
HARRY	So I happen to like weddings.
MAX	He likes weddings, but he loathes marriage.
HARRY	Now I just go to other people's.
GRETA	(wide-eyed) What happened to your wives?
HARRY	They walked out on me.
SYLVIA	I bet you held the door.

HARRY	Can I help it if I'm a gentleman?
GRETA	Three times married and three times divorced?
SYLVIA	Harry always was a man of routine.
GRETA	Didn't you like any of them?
HARRY	'Course I liked them. Liked them all. Carried them over the threshold, didn't I?
GRETA	(warmly) Oh, how romantic!
MAX	Even Brenda?
HARRY	Yes. Even her!
MAX	I thought you'd have needed help with that one. I was waiting round the corner with a fork-lift truck.
HARRY	(laughing) Yes - but I managed - alone!
SYLVIA	So you should. You'd had practice before Brenda. Was she Number Two or Number Three?
HARRY	I don't remember the running order. Only what they cost me. She was the thousand-pound-a-year one.
GRETA	If you liked them, why didn't you keep them?
HARRY	All the girls I married were like Jekyll and Hyde. Outside of marriage they were great. Lovely - nice girls - all of them. Weren't they, Max?
MAX	You always were a good picker, Harry.
HARRY	But once inside - I dunno - you close the door, turn around - and suddenly they have turned into wives. (He says 'wives' like 'monsters'.)
GRETA	So you learned your lesson?
HARRY	You bet. The only girl to marry is a single girl. The trouble is as soon as you marry them they aren't single any more.
GRETA	Weren't you sad when they went?
HARRY	Glad? Of course I was glad!
SYLVIA	Sad! The girl said 'sad'.

A BIRD IN THE HAND

HARRY
: Oh. Yes. I was sad, too. Wouldn't you be? Every time one of them went, my standard of living changed. Do you know how much I pay out in maintenance? (Rising to C.)

SYLVIA
: Harry - she wasn't talking about money.

HARRY
: Oh. (To GRETA.) Weren't you?

SYLVIA
: She thought you might have cried a little.

HARRY
: Cried? I cry enough with my accountant. (To her.) You know something, Miss Ferguson? Before marriage I was a man of property. That right, Max?

MAX
: That's right! He had a big house in Weybridge, a luxury flat in Shepherd Market and a bungalow by the sea.

HARRY
: You know what happened? Number One got Weybridge, Number Two the flat, and Number Three moved to sunny Sussex. What have I got? A basement in Bayswater.

GRETA
: Maybe you just never married the right girl.

HARRY
: Miss Ferguson, once you can make a mistake. Three times - and you know you're a marked man.

GRETA
: So what now? Have you given up girls?

HARRY
: Well - er -

SYLVIA
: He's given up girls like he's given up drink.

HARRY
: You don't stop eating just because you never own a restaurant. (He refills his own glass at the table D.L.)

(PERCH returns from the kitchen, sombrely.)

PERCH
: I've seen to the food, sir. Will there be anything else?

MAX
: No, thank you, Perch. You'd better get back to your lifts.

(PERCH goes above the sofa and pauses to look at HARRY, rather sadly.)

PERCH
: All off now, I suppose? The party and all that.

HARRY
: Looks like it, Perch.

SYLVIA
: Of course it's not off. The boys will still be coming.

PERCH
: Seems to 've rather lost its point, now - nothing much to celebrate now - if you'll pardon the plain speaking, madam.

SYLVIA   Of course there is! Mr. Winton and I are still getting divorced.

PERCH   (brightening) You are, madam? Oh - well, that's different! I am delighted. Thank you, madam. Thank you, sir. Thank you, all! (He goes out, beaming.)

SYLVIA   I think you have a prospective member of your club there, Harry.

HARRY   Yes. All he needs is some courage.

SYLVIA   (rising) Well, come along, Greta. It's time you and I saw about the food. We mustn't prevail on these old bachelors any longer. (GRETA joins her and they move R.)

MAX   Sylvia, you don't have to -

SYLVIA   It's all laid on!

HARRY   We were going out to eat -

SYLVIA   Well, now you don't have to, do you? It'll be much cosier here. (She and GRETA go out R.)

(HARRY turns to look at MAX disapprovingly. MAX cowers a little.)

MAX   I know! I know! I should have taken the latchkey.

HARRY   Ah, what's the difference? She'd have climbed in through the window, anyway. (Moving D.C., thoughtfully, looking towards the door R.) I wonder why she came back.

MAX   You heard her - to look after me until we get divorced.

HARRY   (eagerly, to below R. of sofa) You don't suppose she's going to give up the magazine?

MAX   No. She'd never do that. She keeps telling me how she built that paper up from nothing. Y'know, sometimes I think she loves it more than she ever loved me.

HARRY   (sitting R. of **MAX**) Oh, come on, now - I was your best man, remember? You two were so much in love it was embarrassing.

MAX   I just think a woman should spend more time at home than at the office! Is that so unreasonable?

HARRY	Don't yell at me - I'm on your side. I just want to know why she really came back.
MAX	Well, whatever it was - she's not staying!
HARRY	Looks pretty settled to me.
MAX	(frustrated) But when she left last night it was all agreed. I told her I never wanted to see her again.
HARRY	She must have misunderstood.
MAX	I was firm, Harry - I was firm! You'd have been proud of me. I even surprised myself. I stood right up to her and I said, 'Sylvia', I said -
HARRY	That was a good beginning.
MAX	'Sylvia', I said, 'this is it! The end of the road! Get out of my flat and out of my life!' Pretty good, eh?
HARRY	Great.
MAX	And she stood in the doorway - I can see her now - she stood just there and said, 'Are you sure you mean this, Max?' And I said, 'You're darn right I mean it!' I was firm, Harry. I told her to go - and out she went! (He smiles, remembering with delight.)
HARRY	(after a pause) For twenty-four hours.
MAX	(sobering) Yes. For twenty-four hours. Still - it was a start, Harry. It was a start.
HARRY	Yes. Who knows? In six months' time you might even send her away for two whole days. But by then she will have have eaten you alive.
MAX	(smiling) You know, sometimes I think you know nothing about women.
HARRY	You are speaking to a veteran of three wars. And when you've been under fire like that, you get to know the way the female mind works.
	(MAX laughs.)
MAX	Oh, come on, Harry! They were nice girls you married - all of them. I bet you sometimes they still think about you.

HARRY	Yes - they think about me! They have that in common. The first of the month and they're all thinking about me! And if I'm a week overdue with the cheque they start talking about legal action.
MAX	(dreamily) Sylvia'll never do that.
HARRY	Do what?
MAX	Chase me for money. She's not that kind of girl.
HARRY	Max, you're a dreamer.
MAX	She just wouldn't do it!
HARRY	Max, there are three stages with women - girl-friend, wife and ex-wife. And, believe me, by the time Stage One becomes Stage Three, there has been a complete metamorphosis. Only unlike nature it has worked in reverse - the pretty butterfly has become a grub again.
MAX	(laughing) I just don't believe it! (He rises to get a drink.)
HARRY	Neither did I. I had to go through it all three times before I was convinced.
MAX	If what you say is true, how can you still be interested in girls?
HARRY	Have you found a better alternative? I may not like Stages Two and Three, but I still love the butterflies.
MAX	(romantically) When Sylvia and I get divorced, it'll be friendly. Friendly and civilised. You see.
HARRY	You want me to call my bookie?
	(They both laugh.)
	Anyhow, talking of butterflies, what are we going to do about the girls?
MAX	The girls out there?
HARRY	No, not the girls out there. The girls in here.
MAX	(to L. of sofa) What girls in here?
HARRY	Max, what's the matter with you? The girls who are coming over!

MAX   There aren't any girls coming over. You only said you'd asked a few of the boys.

HARRY   I'm not sitting here holding your hand, that's for sure!

MAX   (alarmed)   You - you didn't ask some girls?

HARRY   (imitating him)   Yes - yes - I did ask some girls. Is that such a terrible idea? You rang me up - told me the good news - and said you wanted some company.

MAX   Your company. I said I was a bachelor again.

HARRY   You didn't say you were celibate. In fact, I seem to remember you even said something about being a loose man looking for loose women.

MAX   That was a joke, Harry!

HARRY   Well, it's too late. They're on their way.

MAX   How many?

HARRY   One each. Don't let's get greedy.

MAX   And no other fellers?

HARRY   What do you want? An audience?

MAX   Just the four of us?

HARRY   Yes. I thought that would be a nice round number. You know - two of each kind.

(MAX crosses to D.C.)

MAX   You'll have to put them off.

HARRY   (rising to him)   I thought you wanted some action.

MAX   Not to-night. Look, I told Sylvia this was going to be a quiet sort of evening - old friends having a drink and discussing life.

HARRY   The girls don't have to talk. They can just sit here. We can look at them and talk to each other. Then if we run out of conversation, there's always something else to do.

MAX   But Sylvia and Miss Ferguson are out there!

HARRY   We can get rid of them.

A BIRD IN THE HAND   Act 1

MAX   That wouldn't make any difference. I can't have girls in here. This is our house - Sylvia's and mine.

(HARRY breaks away to D.L.C.)

HARRY   Now don't start getting all romantic! You've broken up. You're getting divorced!

MAX   No, Harry - you'll have to ring them up and put them off.

HARRY   I can't do that.

MAX   Why not?

HARRY   I don't know where they live. I found them in a bar.

MAX   (to him) Will you stop clowning around? Ring up those girls and put them off.

HARRY   It's too late. They'll be here in a minute.

MAX   What are we going to do?

HARRY   I don't know about you, but first of all I'm going to have another drink - (He starts to replenish his drink.) - and then, with your permission, I'm going to have a quick shave -

MAX   (to him) We've got to stop them! Head them off. We can't have them coming in here, face to face with Sylvia.

HARRY   Max, will you stop bouncing about? You and Sylvia have broken up. You are, therefore, a free man. She can't expect you to behave like a monk.

MAX   But if she finds me here with a girl - the first night after we've separated - how's that going to look to the judge?

(HARRY checks. It's his kind of argument.)

HARRY   Yes. Just think what that could do to the alimony. Okay, Max. Maybe you're right. We'd better head them off. And I thought this was going to be a party -

(They start to go. HARRY returns, picks up a bottle of whisky.)

MAX   What's that for?

HARRY   We could be out there a long time.

(They go out quickly.)

(SYLVIA and GRETA come in from the door D.R. SYLVIA to R. of sofa.)

SYLVIA   Well! Turn your back for two minutes and they run away.

GRETA   Perhaps they went out for a drink.

SYLVIA   There's enough here for an off-licence.

GRETA   Maybe they went to get some coca-cola.

SYLVIA   (grimly) That's likely! (She gets a cigarette from the sofa table and lights it.)

GRETA   Well, I did say I liked it.

SYLVIA   You're talking about Max and Harry. They wouldn't buy coca-cola unless they were giving free whisky away with it.

GRETA   (to L. of the armchair) Oh, I don't think your husband's like that.

SYLVIA   He is when he's with Harry. Once those two have got into their stride, you'd think their lives depended on emptying the bottle.

GRETA   You still love him, though, don't you?

SYLVIA   'Course I love him.

GRETA   So why are you getting divorced?

SYLVIA   (circling to L. of the sofa) Oh, a lot of things. Some my fault, some his. He wants me to give up the magazine - always be here when he comes home. I can understand that. It's what I wanted, too, when we were first married. But now - well, this job's become important to me.

GRETA   Do you often argue about it, then?

SYLVIA   (with a smile) Well - sometimes it's not exactly peaceful co-existence.

GRETA   Yet you still love him?

SYLVIA   I got into the habit of loving him. You can't just turn off twelve years, you know.

GRETA   So that's why you came back?

SYLVIA   You know, for a secretary, you ask too many questions.

GRETA   (a sudden thought)   You don't suppose they've gone for good?

SYLVIA   And left us here with all this booze? You must be joking!

(There is a tap at the door and PERCH comes in. He is somewhat put out at seeing no sign of the men.)

PERCH   Oh! They're not 'ere, then?

SYLVIA   They popped out for a minute.

PERCH   Oh! Popped out, did they? Oh, I see.

SYLVIA   They haven't gone for ever.

PERCH   They must 'ave gone down in my lift.

SYLVIA   Yes - they usually do. It's the quickest way. Unless you're thinking of jumping from the window.

PERCH   They must 'ave gone down in one while we were coming up in the other.

SYLVIA   We?

PERCH   (embarrassed)   Me and the - er - the girls.

SYLVIA   Girls?

PERCH   I'm certain they were girls, madam. Couldn't be no mistake about that.

SYLVIA   What were they like?

PERCH   Pretty good! I mean - they looked all right to me.

SYLVIA   I expect they were going to the next floor. There were some new people moving in up there.

PERCH   No. They were coming 'ere.

SYLVIA   Here?

PERCH   Yes.

SYLVIA   Well, don't leave them standing in the hall, then. Show them in!

A BIRD IN THE HAND

PERCH Oh - yes, madam - yes - right away!   (He hurries out.)

GRETA I thought Mr Tyler had only invited men.

SYLVIA Still dreaming, Greta? When Max and Harry shared a flat in the old days, there were only two things they were interested in - drink and sex. Looks as if they haven't changed.

(PERCH reappears.)

PERCH The young ladies, madam.

(PEGGY and SUE come in. They are two dolly birds of about 18; pretty, mini-skirted and not terribly bright. They stand side by side, looking blankly at SYLVIA and GRETA.)

(PERCH stumbles out, awkwardly.)

SYLVIA Do come in.

(PEGGY and SUE move in, in unison, to R. of the sofa. SYLVIA is D.L. of the sofa; GRETA below the armchair.)

PEGGY Is this the right place?

SYLVIA What place were you looking for?

PEGGY Flat 24.

SYLVIA Then this is the place.

PEGGY Oh.   (Pause.)   It was supposed to be a party.

SYLVIA I expect it'll warm up later. Now - I'm Sylvia, and this is Greta.

PEGGY Hullo.

GRETA How do you do. Shall I take your coats?

PEGGY Oh - all right.

(GRETA takes their coats.)

GRETA (to SYLVIA)   I'll see how the food's getting on.

SYLVIA Oh, thank you. That would be nice.

(GRETA goes out with the coats, after exchanging a smile with SYLVIA.)

Won't you sit down?

PEGGY   Oh - ta.

(The girls sit side by side on the sofa, looking rather apprehensive. SYLVIA is D.L. of the sofa.)

PEGGY   (suddenly)   Sue!

SYLVIA   What?

PEGGY   Sue.

SYLVIA   Oh. How do you do, Sue.

PEGGY   No. She's Sue. I'm Peggy.

SYLVIA   Oh, I see. What would you like to drink? There seems to be practically everything.

PEGGY   Gin and tonic, please.

SUE   Tomato juice.

SYLVIA   Well, that makes a change around here.

(SYLVIA attends to the drinks, her back to the girls. They turn to each other and whisper so that SYLVIA cannot hear.)

SUE   Here! I thought you said there was going to be some fellers?

PEGGY   That's what he said.

SUE   Well, where are they?

PEGGY   I don't know!

SUE   (with dark suspicion)   You don't think it's going to be one of those parties, do you?

PEGGY   No, of course not. Don't be daft.

SUE   'Cos if it is, I'm off. I may be sexy, but I could never be strange.

(SYLVIA brings their drinks.)

SYLVIA   There we are - gin for you, Sue.

PEGGY   I'm Peggy. She's Sue.

SYLVIA   Yes, of course. Sue's the tomato, isn't she?

A BIRD IN THE HAND 33

              (PEGGY and SUE accept their drinks.)

              Well - cheers!

PEGGY   Oh - yes.

SUE   Rather!

              (They drink. There is an awkward pause. The girls shift uneasily. SYLVIA gets a drink for herself.)

PEGGY   I hope nothing's happened to them!

SYLVIA   Who?

PEGGY   Well - er -

SYLVIA   Max and Harry?

PEGGY   Yes.

SYLVIA   I think they're old enough to look after themselves.

              (Another pause.)

PEGGY   I wonder what's holding them up. We thought they'd be here.

SYLVIA   Yes. So did we.

PEGGY   You mean - you and your friend are waiting for them, as well?

SYLVIA   Yes. Aren't they lucky? Two each.

              (PEGGY and SUE exchange a look.)

SUE   Perhaps we'd better be going -

SYLVIA   But you've only just arrived.

SUE   Yes - but - I mean, you were here first.

              (SYLVIA moves above the sofa to R. of it.)

SYLVIA   Good heavens, we're not queueing for a bus! Max and Harry would never forgive me if I let you go now.

PEGGY   Do you suppose there'll be some other fellers? You know - so there's more to go around.

SYLVIA   Oh, I expect so.

SUE Maybe they made a mistake about the date.

PEGGY Yes! Perhaps you were for to-night, and we were for to-morrow!

SYLVIA A sort of rota system?   (Away to the armchair.)

SUE (rising)   They don't sound very nice to me. I'm off!

PEGGY (aside)   Will you stop being so daft?

(SYLVIA sits in the armchair, facing them.)

SYLVIA Now - how did you both meet Mr Tyler?

PEGGY I'm a typist where he works.

SUE And so am I.

PEGGY And so is she. It was last night. I was getting ready to go home, when Harry -   (She gives a little giggle at the familiarity of the name.)   - came in and asked if I'd like to come around and bring a friend. He said he and this friend of his - er -

SYLVIA Max.

PEGGY Yes, that's right. He and Max were having a little celebration, and would we like to come along. So I said yes.

SUE And so did I.

PEGGY And so did she.

SYLVIA Did he happen to say what it was they were celebrating?

PEGGY Not exactly. He just said something about the old girl leaving at last.

SYLVIA (ominously)   Oh, did he?

PEGGY Is that what he said to you?

SYLVIA No, not exactly. You see, Greta and I are only here to see to the food. The party is just for the four of you.

PEGGY They asked you along just to do the cooking? What a nerve!

SYLVIA Well, I've known them a long time, you see.

PEGGY Do you often do this? The cooking, I mean?

SYLVIA	Quite often. More for Max than for Harry. You see - as a matter of fact - Max is my uncle.
SUE	Uncle! (To PEGGY.) I thought you said they were young.
SYLVIA	I expect that was what they said.
PEGGY	I never said they were young. I said they were mature.
SYLVIA	If they don't come in soon they'll be over-ripe.

(PEGGY rises L. of SYLVIA.)

PEGGY	Do they often have girls in to dinner, then?
SYLVIA	Well, I must be honest with you. You're not the first.
PEGGY	You mean they've - got into the habit of it?
SYLVIA	Well, some men play golf - Max and Harry prefer girls.

(SUE leaps up.)

SUE	Here - I'm off.
PEGGY	Don't be so daft!
SUE	I'm not going to be treated like no game!
PEGGY	Do sit down. I'm hungry. If you're going to go, go after dinner.

(Reluctantly SUE sits down again. PEGGY turns once more to SYLVIA.)

What - what kind of girls?

SYLVIA	All kinds - Chinese, Russian, African -
PEGGY	(horrified) You mean they go out with foreign girls?
SYLVIA	Oh, yes. They're very liberal. The Chinese girls were sweet! You should have seen them having dinner - all sitting cross-legged around the coffee table! Come to think of it, they spent most of the evening on the floor.
SUE	(leaping up again) That's it! I've heard enough! (She moves quickly L. PEGGY follows to D.L. of sofa.)
PEGGY	Will you stop bouncing up and down?

36   A BIRD IN THE HAND   Act 1

SUE   They're not getting me on the floor for dinner!
PEGGY   Don't be daft. You're not Chinese, are you?
SUE   I'm not Russian, either, but I'm still going to say 'No'!
           (The front door is heard to slam and the men's voices in the hall.)
SYLVIA   Ah! Here they come!
           (MAX and HARRY come in, talking to each other. They arrive C., stop, react and turn slowly to look at the girls. Then they turn to look at SYLVIA. She smiles broadly, enjoying the situation.)
           Well, it's about time you showed up. The girls have been waiting!
           (MAX and HARRY look slowly back at the girls. SUE is eyeing them warily after what she has heard. HARRY attempts to carry off the situation. He goes to below C. of the sofa.)
HARRY   Hello, girls! So you finally made it?
PEGGY   We've been here for ages.
HARRY   Oh, have you? I'm so sorry. We went out to stop you - er - to meet you.
SYLVIA   You must have just missed each other. Never mind, I gave them both a drink and we've been sitting here - talking.
MAX   (nervously)   Talking?
SYLVIA   Well, we could hardly sit around in silence like a seance, could we?
MAX   Wha - wha - what have you been talking about?
SYLVIA   The Far East.
PEGGY   It was ever so funny. When we first arrived - we thought that they were waiting for you, as well!
MAX   Oh, really? Yes, that must have been funny.
SUE   (to PEGGY)   I think I want to go home.

A BIRD IN THE HAND

PEGGY	(to SUE) Oh, do be quiet! You've only just arrived. (To HARRY.) Aren't you going to introduce us, Harry?
HARRY	I gather you've already met.
PEGGY	Not to her - to him.
HARRY	Oh, yes! This is Max. Max, this is Sue -
SYLVIA	No, Harry - that's Peggy.
HARRY	What?
SYLVIA	The other one's Sue.
HARRY	Yes - that's what I meant.
SYLVIA	Max - you're being introduced.
MAX	I know that!
SYLVIA	Well, shake them by the hand, then.
	(MAX, deeply embarrassed, solemnly shakes hands with SUE and PEGGY.)
MAX	How do you do. How do you do. (He wanders back towards SYLVIA, laughs nervously and turns upstage to R. of the sofa, embarrassed.)
HARRY	Well, come on, girls, sit down. Not going anywhere, are you?
	(They cross and sit on the sofa.)
	Let me get you another drink. (He takes their glasses.) Gin and tonic. And how about you - Bloody Mary?
SUE	No. I'm Sue - she's -
HARRY	(patiently) Your drink. Is that a Bloody Mary?
SUE	(alarmed) Oh, I don't think so.
SYLVIA	Straight tomato juice.
HARRY	(on his way to the drinks table) Tomato juice and coca-cola - some party!
PEGGY	(to SUE, looking at MAX) He's not as old as I thought.

	(SYLVIA enjoys this. MAX glares at her, then turns to PEGGY.)
MAX	What did you expect - the Old Man of the Mountains? It may surprise you to know - I am not yet in line for the pension!
	(HARRY arrives with the drinks.)
HARRY	One gin and tonic, and one straight tomato juice.
SYLVIA	(sweetly) Help yourself, won't you, Harry?
HARRY	I may just do that. How about you, Max? Whisky?
MAX	Just take the top off.
SUE	(eyes popping) Is he going to drink it out of the bottle?
SYLVIA	He always does. It saves the washing up.
MAX	(turning to the girls with a nervous laugh) She's just having a little joke at my expense. She always does that. You know how it is. I - I expect it's just because she's my sister.
PEGGY	Your sister?
MAX	(smiling at his clever subterfuge) That's right.
PEGGY	She said you were her uncle!
	(MAX's smile disappears.)
MAX	She did, eh? (At sea.) Well, I don't know how she came to make a mistake like that -
HARRY	(moving to MAX with drinks) Well, I do. Sylvia has this age complex. She doesn't like anyone to think she's old enough to have a brother looking like him. (To MAX.) Have a whisky, uncle.
	(GRETA comes in R.)
GRETA	Ready when you are!
MAX	What's that?
GRETA	Dinner! Come and get it!
PEGGY	Sylvia was telling us how she and Greta often come in to cook for you.

MAX	Oh, was she?
PEGGY	You're very lucky to have such a kind sister.
MAX	Yes -
SYLVIA	(rising, sweetly) Well, come on boys - take the girls into dinner.
	(HARRY hesitates, gives her a look that could kill, then lumbers off towards the dining-room. The girls get up.)
HARRY	(off-hand) Through here.
SYLVIA	(sorrowfully) Oh, Harry - don't say you've forgotten your manners.
	(Reluctantly he goes back and offers his arm to PEGGY. She giggles and takes it.)
PEGGY	Oo! (She giggles again as they go off past GRETA.)
SYLVIA	Max -
	(He makes a move towards SUE. She backs away.)
SUE	You keep away from me! I've been hearing all about you!
MAX	(looking at SYLVIA) Yes, I bet you have.
SYLVIA	It's all right, Sue. You go along with Max. You'll be quite safe.
SUE	(doubtfully) Well - if you say so - (Warily, she takes MAX's arm.)
SYLVIA	(smiling sweetly at MAX) After all - I shall be there to see he behaves himself.
SUE	All right, then. (As they go.) But don't you try your Chinese nonsense on me.
	(She and MAX go out.)
	(GRETA looks at SYLVIA, who is smiling broadly.)
GRETA	Aren't you angry?
SYLVIA	Angry? Of course not! This is just what I wanted!
	(She offers her arm to GRETA, who takes it. They go off, smiling.)

CURTAIN

ACT TWO

It is an hour later. When the curtain rises, the record player is emitting some bright music. HARRY is below the sofa executing a few steps, snapping his fingers in time to the music. MAX is slumped in the armchair R.C., gazing disconsolately into space, a glass in his hand and the whisky bottle nearby.

HARRY looks at MAX and gradually slows down to a halt as his enthusiasm dies. He walks heavily to the record player, switches it off and sinks despondently onto the sofa with his drink.

HARRY	Fine party this turned out to be. I haven't had such a good time since we buried my grandfather.
MAX	What do you expect - with Sylvia and Miss Ferguson in and out of the room all the time we were eating?
HARRY	Yes. They kept circling the table like two vultures waiting for us to die.
MAX	Do you think the girls enjoyed it?
HARRY	They ate as if they hadn't tasted food for three weeks.

A BIRD IN THE HAND   41

MAX   Maybe they hadn't.

HARRY   Yes. Been out with too many younger fellers. All they'd get from them is coca-cola and 'Come into the Garden, Maud'.

MAX   That's one thing about getting older, Harry - you know how to treat a girl - you know what I mean?

HARRY   Will you stop talking about getting old!

MAX   Older - that's all I said. Older.

HARRY   I am not older than anybody else!

MAX   Forget it. Have another drink.

HARRY   That's the first sensible thing you've said.   (He comes across for a refill.)   It was a great meal.

MAX   (romantically)   Yes. You know, I'd almost forgotten what a good cook Sylvia was.

HARRY   She still is.

MAX   That's what I mean. Great cook.

HARRY   Max, you don't have to marry someone just because she is a good cook. I know thousands of girls who are good cooks, but I haven't married them all.

MAX   You made a start.

HARRY   Well, take some advice, then, from a man who has married three cooks. It is cheaper to go to a restaurant.
         (Returns to the sofa.)

MAX   She doesn't love me.

HARRY   Who?

MAX   Sylvia, of course.

HARRY   (mildly sarcastic)   Now what makes you say that? Just because you're getting divorced?

MAX   No, no - not just that.

HARRY   What, then?

MAX   She wasn't even angry. Why didn't she throw those girls out of here?

HARRY   Because it's your flat, that's why.

MAX   That wasn't the reason. It was because she doesn't love me. She doesn't care.

HARRY   No, Max. It's because she's a civilised woman.

MAX   No, she is not! I won't have you say that about Sylvia. She is not a civilised woman!

HARRY   What is she, then?

MAX   (after a moment's thought)   She is a human being.

HARRY   Yes. A human being who can cook.

(There is a pause as they both consider the profundity of this. They take a drink.)

MAX   Not once.

HARRY   Not once what?

MAX   Not once did she look angry. Throughout the whole meal all she did was - smile.

HARRY   Max, when a woman is smiling she's at her most dangerous.

MAX   You think so?

HARRY   I'm telling you. All my wives were great smilers. Anyhow, what do you care?

MAX   What do you mean?

HARRY   Does it matter whether Sylvia loves you?

MAX   Of course it matters!

HARRY   But you're getting divorced!

MAX   I know that.

HARRY   So what difference does it make whether Sylvia loves you or not?

MAX   You don't understand, Harry. I could never divorce a woman who didn't love me!   (Pause.)   Can you imagine how I felt sitting there eating a meal with two girls - and all the time my wife watching - and smiling?

HARRY   Yes -

A BIRD IN THE HAND   43

MAX   Why was she smiling?

HARRY   Well, either she's smiling because she loves you, or she's smiling because she doesn't love you. If she's smiling because she loves you, it means she's saving up her wrath for later. And if she's smiling because she doesn't love you, it means that in her mind's eye she is already looking at her bank statement!

MAX   Harry, you've been married three times and you know nothing about women.

HARRY   I know now not to marry them.

(MAX rises carefully and wanders to HARRY with his drink and the bottle.)

MAX   How long were you married - h'm?

HARRY   Collectively?

MAX   One at a time.

HARRY   Five years. Three years. Eighteen months. The sentences got shorter.

MAX   So - after three marriages your sum total of married experience is less than mine.

HARRY   So what does that prove? Either that you're more tolerant than I am, or that I'm just quicker at getting away.

MAX   Have another drink.   (He refills their glasses.)

HARRY   You're not weakening, are you?

MAX   What d'you mean?

HARRY   Getting cold feet. Having second thoughts. About Sylvia leaving, I mean.

MAX   Oh, no! Never! I am going through with it, all right. Maybe I am more tolerant than you, Harry. Maybe it has taken me a long time to decide. But I have decided! Sylvia and I are going to be divorced. There is no turning back, no re-thinking. We are parting for good - for ever! But is that any reason why she shouldn't love me?

HARRY   All right, then, if you still intend to divorce her, will you please ask her to get the hell out of here? She's cramping my style with the girls!

A BIRD IN THE HAND   Act II

MAX   (without too much conviction)   Okay, Harry - I'll get her to go.   (He sits down beside HARRY.)

HARRY   Now?

MAX   I'll - I'll get around to it.

HARRY   You'll get around to it. Look, the night is still young. There is still time for us all to enjoy ourselves. There's plenty of booze, we can have music on the record player and there are two pretty girls powdering their noses in the ladies' room. The evening is full of potential. But there is one small drawback, one dark cloud hanging over us - your wife is still here! So will you please - just for my sake, if you've lost your enthusiasm - but will you please ask her to go?

MAX   Okay, Harry. Okay. I'll ask her.   (He rises, starting to go, but turns back vaguely.)   Where is she?

HARRY   She's out there - smiling - and helping the girls with the washing-up!

MAX   I thought you said they were powdering their noses.

HARRY   That was a figure of speech, Max.

MAX   Couldn't Sylvia and Miss Ferguson manage the dishes alone?

HARRY   Isn't that just what I said in there? Isn't that what I said? But Peggy and Sue - they just insisted. You know, it's a funny thing, but those girls seem to actually like your wife.

MAX   Yes, I know. That's what makes it worse.   (He sits next to HARRY on the sofa.)   'Course I can understand it. She's a very likeable kind of woman.

HARRY   Please, Max - no! She is going!

(PEGGY and SUE come in. The wine at dinner has made PEGGY rather giggly. MAX remains in his gloom. HARRY rises and tries to gay up the proceedings.)

Well, hello, girls! Come on in. Let me get you a drink. Max, the girls are here.

(MAX does not react. The girls move to D.R.C.)

What'll it be? Liqueur? Brandy?

A BIRD IN THE HAND 45

PEGGY   Could I have one of those little green drinks?

HARRY   You like that flavour, eh?

PEGGY   Oh, no! But I love the colour.

HARRY   How about you, Sue?

SUE   Tomato juice, please.

HARRY   You going to drink tomato juice all the evening?

SUE   (defensively)   I like it. It's good for me.

HARRY   You'll end up being the healthiest person in the room. Max, will you wake up? The girls are here!   (He goes to the drinks table.)

MAX   (coming to)   Oh - oh, yes. Hullo, girls.   (He rises.)   You going to have a drink?

HARRY   We've just been through all that. Where were you?

MAX   Would you - would you like to sit down?

PEGGY   Thanks.   (She and SUE sit down on the sofa.)
I hope we didn't wake you.

MAX   No, No, I was just dreaming - you know.

PEGGY   (without rancour)   I mean, I know men quite often like to doze off after a meal when they get to your age.

MAX   Peggy, I realise this may be hard for you to believe, but because a man is over thirty -

HARRY   Thirty - ha!

MAX   - it does not necessarily follow that he is no longer in possession of his faculties.   (He crosses moodily above the sofa to U.C.)

PEGGY   Oh, I didn't mean it like that.   (She makes a face at SUE.)   What have I said?

(HARRY arrives with the drinks.)

HARRY   Here we are - one red one for you, and one green one for you. How about that, eh?

(MAX wanders down to R. of the sofa. He still has the bottle and his own drink.)

PEGGY	Thanks.	
SUE	Ta.	
PEGGY	(saucily) I wonder if these colours mean anything.	
HARRY	What's that?	
PEGGY	Well – (Indicating SUE's drink.) red for stop, and (Indicating her own.) green for go! (She giggles.)	
	(The men exchange a pained look.)	
SUE	If they do, I'm glad I've got the red one.	
HARRY	You know, you don't say much, but when you do – my God, it has point.	
PEGGY	Cheers!	
	(They drink. SUE reacts.)	
SUE	Here! Have you put something in this?	
HARRY	I just waved the vodka bottle over it.	
SUE	Are you trying to get me drunk?	
HARRY	Whatever gave you that idea?	
SUE	I just wondered.	
HARRY	It freshens the tomato juice up a little.	
PEGGY	It was a lovely meal.	
MAX	(dreamily) Yes. Sylvia always was a good cook.	
HARRY	(quickly) Yes – for a sister she's a great cook.	
PEGGY	Quite handy, really.	
HARRY	What is?	
PEGGY	Having her around when you and Max do your – entertaining. (She imbues the word with sinister overtones.)	
HARRY	Oh, yes – sure! (Puzzled, he looks at MAX and shrugs.)	

A BIRD IN THE HAND 47

SUE	Nice for the girls, too. At least there's somebody there if they want to call for help.
HARRY	The girls we entertain don't usually need any help.
PEGGY	(giggling) What about you and those Chinese girls, eh, Harry?
HARRY	It may surprise you to know that Max and I know nothing at all about Chinese girls.
PEGGY	Oh, yes, you do! Sylvia told us all about it. You spent half the evening on the floor!
	(MAX does the nose trick.)
SUE	Have you taken out a lot of foreign girls?
MAX	Millions. Harry used to work for the United Nations. (He slumps into the armchair.)
HARRY	(to change the subject) Let's have a little music - what do you say?
PEGGY	Oh, yes - lovely!
	(HARRY goes and turns on the record player. Slow music, 1940 vintage, a waltz like 'Apple Blossom Time'. HARRY hums the tune and moves in time to the music to R. of the sofa.)
HARRY	Okay - you want to dance?
PEGGY	To that?
HARRY	Yes.
PEGGY	What is it?
HARRY	What do you mean what is it?
PEGGY	What kind of a dance do you do to it?
HARRY	(getting a little angry) You do a waltz! What do you think you do? Come on!
PEGGY	(with a giggle) I wouldn't know what to do.
HARRY	Just follow me.
PEGGY	I couldn't!

HARRY	I'll have you know, I learned to dance with Arthur Murray and my waltz is second to none!
PEGGY	Could you dance to this, Sue?
SUE	(appalled) Oo, no!
	(PEGGY rises and goes to turn the music off.)
HARRY	What's the matter with you girls? It's a nice, romantic tune.
SUE	It's too slow.
PEGGY	Let's have something a bit more lively. (She searches amongst the records.) Nobody dances to that sort of thing nowadays.
	(MAX and HARRY remain immobile, accepting the bludgeons of the age gap.)
	Haven't you got anything else?
HARRY	(drily) We may have a little Chinese boogie-woogie.
PEGGY	(finding something) Ah, here we are! This'll be better.
HARRY	Don't say we actually have something acceptable.
PEGGY	Now - you see the difference!
	(She puts the new record on. It is a violent, noisy, modern top of the pops.)
	Come on, then!
	(She pulls HARRY, plus his drink, from which he refuses to be parted, into the centre of the room. She dances around him wildly.)
HARRY	You call this dancing? You're not anywhere near me.
	(SUE rises and goes to MAX.)
SUE	You want to dance?
MAX	(alarmed) What?
SUE	Well, you can't go to sleep again with this on, can you?

A BIRD IN THE HAND

(MAX reluctantly follows her to below the sofa, taking his glass and the bottle with him. The girls dance wildly round the men, who remain for the most part immobile in the middle. They look at each other and shrug as they find themselves together in the midst of the whirling miniskirts. MAX solemnly refills both their glasses and they drink as the girls dance on.

(SYLVIA comes in. She is wearing an apron over her dress and carries a tray. The men see her and freeze. She smiles broadly. They smile back, like two boys caught stealing the apples. HARRY turns off the music and moves D.L.)

SYLVIA   Oh, please don't turn it off. It's so nice to see you young people enjoying yourselves. Put it on again, please, Sue.

SUE   Oh, okay.   (She turns it on again - only quieter this time so as not to drown the dialogue - and the girls continue to dance upstage.)

SYLVIA   Don't let me interrupt you boys.   (With a sweet smile she crosses to the drinks table.)   I just came to collect the glasses.

HARRY   Sylvia - the party is not yet over.

SYLVIA   I know that, Harry. But I thought, while I was at it, I might as well wash up the dirty glasses.

HARRY   We are using the dirty glasses.

SYLVIA   Don't be silly. The place is full of them.   (She starts to put dirty glasses onto a tray.)   What's the matter with Max?

(MAX is still immobile, below the sofa.)

HARRY   I think it is conceivable that your presence may be hampering his freedom of action.

SYLVIA   (innocently)   Good heavens, why?   (She moves to MAX.)   Max, are you feeling all right?

MAX   Me? Yes - I'm fine. Just fine.

SYLVIA   (gently)   These girls will think you're an awful drag if you just stand about like that, you know. Come on - loosen up a little.

MAX	Sylvia, will you please get out of here?
SYLVIA	Yes, of course, but I've got to tidy up, haven't I? After all, you'd be furious in the morning if you found the place cluttered with dirty dishes. You know what you're like. (She prepares to leave.) But I mustn't stop you boys dancing. Now, come on, Max. You're always telling me how good you used to be at the Palais Glide. (She makes for the door R.)
	(PEGGY moves quickly to SYLVIA. SUE turns off the music.)
PEGGY	You're not going, are you, Sylvia?
SYLVIA	Well, I have a few things still to do in the kitchen.
PEGGY	Oh, no! You've done enough for one night.
HARRY	(aside) Yes, she certainly has.
	(SUE to between MAX and HARRY.)
PEGGY	After cooking that beautiful meal you ought to be sitting down and being looked after. Isn't that right, Sue?
SUE	Oh, yes - rather. It was a lovely meal.
PEGGY	Max, how can you let your sister go on working like this? It's just not fair. I don't think you appreciate her.
SYLVIA	Well, you know what brothers are like.
MAX	It was her idea, anyway.
HARRY	Yes - we didn't ask her to cook.
PEGGY	How can you be so ungrateful? Here, you give me that. (She takes the tray.)
	(SUE goes to join PEGGY.)
SYLVIA	No, please, I -
PEGGY	Give it to me! Here you are, Sue. (She hands the tray to SUE.) If there's any work to be done around here - we'll do it. Now, you come over here - (She leads SYLVIA to the sofa.) - and sit right down for the rest of the evening.

A BIRD IN THE HAND   51

(MAX gives to R. of the sofa.)

SYLVIA No - really - I'd much rather -

PEGGY   We insist! Don't we, Sue?

SUE   Yes - rather.

PEGGY   So you sit there.   (She puts SYLVIA down.)
        Harry, get a drink for Sylvia.

HARRY   A drink?

PEGGY   A large brandy.

HARRY   But I -

PEGGY   (loudly)   Harry!

        (HARRY obediently goes to pour a brandy.)

        Now, you just sit back there and relax and leave everything
        else to me and Sue. It won't take us a minute.   (Going
        to the door.)   And you two can say thank you very
        much for a nice dinner! We'll soon finish off these glasses.

        (They go out, chattering like magpies. The minute they
        have gone there is a loud crash as SUE drops the tray.
        Slowly the door re-opens and SUE looks in.)

MAX   (without moving)   You'll find the dustpan and brush in
        the first cupboard on the left.

        (SUE goes out.)

SYLVIA What sweet girls!

HARRY   Yes. Cute.

SYLVIA How you two old fogies managed to pick them up, I don't
        know.

MAX   We did not pick them up.

SYLVIA Oh, you mean they just arrived on the doorstep with the
        milk.

HARRY   Brandy.

SYLVIA What? Oh - thank you -   (She takes the brandy.)

HARRY	Did you hear the way that girl bawled at me? Did you hear that? It's sad, I tell you.	
SYLVIA	What's sad about it?	
HARRY	She's only eighteen years old - and already she has the makings of a wife!	
SYLVIA	I wonder where they all ended up.	
MAX	Who?	
SYLVIA	The other men. The ones Harry said were coming over tonight. They must have lost their way.	
MAX	Oh - them! Yes. Well, they - they rang up. Didn't you hear the phone? They couldn't make it.	
SYLVIA	None of them?	
MAX	No.	
SYLVIA	Not even one each for Miss Ferguson and me?	
HARRY	Is she still here?	
SYLVIA	Oh, yes. She's typing in the bedroom.	
HARRY	She's been typing ever since we started the dessert! What's she working on? 'War and Peace' ?	
	(HARRY looks at MAX and indicates his wristwatch.)	
HARRY	Okay, Max - er - time's getting on - h'm?	
MAX	What's that?	
HARRY	(pointedly) It is getting late. The evening may not be ours for ever. (He indicates to get SYLVIA out of here, a mime that does not escape her notice.)	
MAX	Oh. Oh, yes. Yes. (He turns to SYLVIA.) Er - Sylvia - do you suppose that you - and Miss Ferguson - could - well - I know this is a difficult thing to ask - I mean, you live here and all that - or rather you did live here - but not any more! - no, not any more! So, if you - and Miss Ferguson - could - well, if you could - (He is floundering hopelessly.)	
SYLVIA	Are you asking me to go?	

MAX	Er - well, yes. You could put it that way.
SYLVIA	But I'm enjoying myself.
MAX	Yes - but we weren't actually thinking about you, Sylvia. How can I put this?
HARRY	Tell her to get to hell out of here!
SYLVIA	I'm not in the way, am I?
MAX	Look, Sylvia, I'll try to explain -
HARRY	What's to explain?
MAX	Harry, will you be quiet for two minutes? (He sits beside SYLVIA and takes her hands.) Sylvia - yesterday you and I decided to call it a day - yes?
SYLVIA	Yes. I remember that.
MAX	We decided to go our separate ways.
SYLVIA	Yes.
MAX	This was no hasty decision. We had considered it carefully.
HARRY	Yes - for twelve years!
MAX	(ignoring this) But in the end we had come to the conclusion that - well, maybe we were better apart.
HARRY	What are you telling her all this for? She was there!
MAX	Harry!
	(HARRY shrugs and pours another drink.)
	So yesterday you packed your things - and we said goodbye - and you left the flat. From that moment, Sylvia, I was a free man. You understand? Free to live my own life in my own way. Free to go out with any girl I choose! But then - you came back. Now, how can a man entertain a girl if his wife's there all the time? It makes you feel so silly. As if you were a kid.
SYLVIA	I suppose it was rather thoughtless of me.
MAX	Well, yes - that's what I felt!
SYLVIA	Except, of course, I am still your wife.

54 A BIRD IN THE HAND Act II

MAX That's only a matter of time. We're only waiting for the law to take its course.

SYLVIA But you haven't even filled in the forms yet -

MAX Tomorrow. I told you. I'm doing it tomorrow. So - if you wouldn't mind - it would sort of ease the situation if you - and Miss Ferguson - and her typewriter - were all to - well, to leave. Now, what do you say?

SYLVIA (after a pause) No.

(MAX rises.)

MAX (loudly) What do you mean 'No'?

HARRY Yes - what do you mean 'No'?

SYLVIA It wouldn't be fair on you.

MAX On me? How do you make that out?

SYLVIA I came back to look after you, Max. Isn't that what you wanted?

MAX Oh, no! I want a full-time wife. Not a part-time one.

SYLVIA Isn't it better to have half a wife who looks after you than no wife at all.

MAX I don't need looking after! (He turns away to face R.)

SYLVIA Oh, yes, you do. You're hopeless about the house. That's why you need me. You never remember where you put things. I've never known you able to find the right shirt - and as for socks! (To HARRY.) I remember once he looked for over an hour for his cuff links, and then found they were in his shirt all the time. (To MAX.) That's another of the reasons I'm leaving you - I simply couldn't bear it any longer!

(MAX turns to her.)

MAX All right, then, why don't you go?

SYLVIA And leave you to struggle on all on your own? It's unthinkable! You've convinced me of that. And now I know I couldn't possibly leave you until you've made other arrangements.

A BIRD IN THE HAND 55

MAX — Sylvia, how can we go on living together when we're separated?

SYLVIA — It's purely a business arrangement, darling. You let me have an office in your flat, in return for which I do the cooking.

HARRY — Max, don't listen to this woman. Look what happened here tonight. It would be like that every time you invited a girl back. Sylvia would be there, cooking and smiling - and messing up your evening!

(SYLVIA rises and gives her empty glass to HARRY.)

SYLVIA — Harry, your experience of marriage has soured you. Some people are still capable of behaving in a civilised manner. Aren't they, Max?

(MAX is now in a state of indecisive dither.)

MAX — Will you stop confusing me! (He turns away R.) You know how long it takes me to make up my mind about something. Twelve years this took! Twelve years to decide our marriage was no good. But I have decided, and we are not going back on it!

SYLVIA — Nobody's arguing about that, darling. It's simply a question of the catering.

HARRY — (with great magnanimity) All right - I tell you what. I'll move in with Max. How about that, eh?

SYLVIA — You?

HARRY — Yes. Why not?

SYLVIA — You'll find his shirts for him? And his cuff links?

HARRY — Well, I -

SYLVIA — (crossing to MAX) And sew on his buttons? And mend his socks?

(MAX squirms uneasily.)

HARRY — We always managed in the old days. Didn't we, Max?

MAX — Of course we did!

SYLVIA — Oh, yes - but the place was full of girls in those days.

56   A BIRD IN THE HAND   Act II

HARRY It'll be no different now.

SYLVIA You want a bet?

HARRY (to below L. end of the sofa)   Look - I have only to lift the phone and the place will be full of seamstresses. And pretty ones, too.

SYLVIA I'm glad you think so.

HARRY I know so! How about those two girls tonight? That wasn't bad for starters, was it?

SYLVIA You don't think that, after a while, they'd find you a bit on the slow side?

HARRY (laughing)   You hear that, Max? You and me - slow! How about that?

SYLVIA After all, you don't even dance the way they do.

HARRY Then we'll find something else to do.

MAX (below SYLVIA to her L.)   Yes - we'll manage all right - you see!

SYLVIA (thoughtfully)   H'm. Perhaps you will. After all, I suppose you could always ring the W.V.S.

HARRY Very funny.   (He gets a drink.)

SYLVIA (as he lifts the bottle)   Have a drink, Harry.

HARRY It happens to be my booze!

SYLVIA Which one of you will do the cooking?

MAX We always used to take it in turns.

SYLVIA (to HARRY)   Then I'll have to leave you the diet sheets. (She moves upstage a little.)

HARRY Diet sheets?

SYLVIA For Max. He can't eat everything, you know.

HARRY (slightly alarmed)   Why not?

MAX (embarrassed)   Well, it's - it's this digestive trouble I've got.   (He sits R. end of the sofa.)

HARRY You mean you're a sick man?

A BIRD IN THE HAND

MAX   Oh, no - no, not sick, Harry. Not sick. I just have to be careful - you know. If - er - If I eat anything very rich, I - I get this kind of a pain -

HARRY   Pain?

MAX   Not much, mind you - but I do feel it.

HARRY   Whereabouts do you feel it?

(MAX unbuttons his shirt as he talks to indicate the area of his diaphragm.)

MAX   Well, it's - er - it's just about here. Just there - you see? It doesn't last long - nothing like that. But it is there. So I have to watch it. You know what I mean?

HARRY   But that's just what I have.

(MAX looks at him in horrified surprise. SYLVIA can hardly contain her laughter.)

MAX   You?

HARRY   Yes.   (He sits beside MAX and unbuttons his shirt.) It - it gets me about there. Just there. Do you see? Is that the same area as you?

(They compare areas.)

MAX   Yes - that's it! The same spot!

HARRY   Sort of a sharp pain? Like a knife?

MAX   Yes! So you've got it, too?

HARRY   Had it for a year now. That's why I gave up eating curry.

SYLVIA   (laughing)   If you could only see yourselves now! The sex symbols of the 1970's!

(She laughs at them as they sit, side by side, forlornly comparing their naked diaphragms. They react to her, and at that moment PEGGY and SUE return from the kitchen. They stand aghast at the spectacle before them. The men rise and hastily button up their shirts. SYLVIA is now U.R. of the sofa, the girls below the armchair. HARRY away to D.L.)

PEGGY   What on earth are you doing?

MAX	We were just comparing.	
HARRY	Max said he was slimmer than me.	
PEGGY	Oh. And who won?	
SYLVIA	The judge declared 'No Contest'.	
HARRY	(deliberately changing the subject) You finished the washing-up, then, girls?	
PEGGY	(sternly) Yes. We did. And that's not all.	
HARRY	What's the matter? Something on your mind?	
PEGGY	Sue - show him.	

(SUE produces a photograph from behind her back, crosses to MAX below the sofa and holds it out to him.)

SUE	It's a photograph.
MAX	(taking it) Oh, yes, you're right. It's a - (As he sees what it is he throws a frantic look at HARRY.) - it's a photograph. What about it?
PEGGY	It's a picture of a wedding.

(He stares blankly at her.)

MAX	A wedding?
SYLVIA	Two people getting married.
SUE	Do you recognise anybody?
MAX	Er - no. No, I can't say I do. (He goes to HARRY.) Harry, do you recognise anyone in this - er - picture of a wedding?
HARRY	Looks a pretty repulsive couple to me.
SUE	(to MAX) One of them is you - and the other one is her! (Pointing to SYLVIA.)
MAX	One of them is me? Let me have a look at that thing. No, you must be mistaken.
SUE	(pointing) There! That one - that man - that's you! (To SYLVIA.) You're not his sister, are you?

A BIRD IN THE HAND

PEGGY	Or his niece!
SUE	You're his wife!
HARRY	Game, set and match.
PEGGY	You never said you were married, did you? You never told us!
MAX	It - it just never came up.
SUE	(to HARRY)　　And what about you?
HARRY	(slightly alarmed)　　You haven't found a picture of me, have you?
SUE	Are you married too?
	(SYLVIA is enjoying the situation.)
HARRY	Oh, no. I have been but I gave it up.
MAX	He 'has-been' three times! At least I only married once.
HARRY	Yes, but my 'has-been-three-times' beats your 'is-once'.
PEGGY	How could you do it?
MAX	Do what?
PEGGY	How could you humiliate that woman - ?
	(PEGGY and SUE cross upstage to SYLVIA, making comforting noises, one on each side of her.)
	Poor Sylvia - what a dreadful thing to live through!
SUE	Dreadful - quite dreadful!
PEGGY	She's a wonderful woman to have put up with you -
SUE	Wonderful - just wonderful!
PEGGY	It's absolutely awful the way you've treated her -
SUE	Awful - just awful!
PEGGY	Inviting girls into your flat - and all the time your poor wife sitting there and - suffering!

(The girls cling onto SYLVIA, making suitable sympathetic noises.)

(The men are D.L.)

(PERCH comes in, reacts to the scene and goes straight out again.)

SYVLIA   Sue! Peggy! Please - You don't understand - Max and I are getting divorced.

PEGGY   And after what's happened tonight, I don't blame you! Now, you come along with us, Sylvia. You're not staying here a moment longer with these two - animals!

SUE   Yes, that's right - we'll look after you -

(They are leading SYLVIA across to the door R.)

PEGGY   You get your things together - we'll take you home with us. (To the men.) You ought to be ashamed of yourselves!

(They go out with SYLVIA, still clucking sympathetically over her.

(The men are left in a vacuum. HARRY, like a homing pigeon, makes for the booze. MAX sinks onto the sofa. He pours two stiff ones and crosses to MAX, who automatically puts out a hand to accept the glass. They drink in silence. MAX is gazing dreamily at the wedding picture.)

HARRY   You see what I mean? To look at those girls in the office, you'd never think that if you wrapped them up and took them home they'd turn into monsters. (He looks at MAX.) What's the matter?

MAX   H'm? Oh - er - I was just - just looking at this picture - you know. Only seems the other day. Y'know - we weren't a bad-looking couple - (He smiles happily, remembering.)

HARRY   (peering at the picture) Well, at least you were prettier in those days.

(A tap at the door and PERCH looks in.)

A BIRD IN THE HAND

PERCH   All clear now, sir?

MAX   Oh, come on in, Perch.

PERCH   (to R. of sofa)   I looked in before, but the young ladies were carrying on a bit so I went out again.

MAX   Oh - yes.

PERCH   Rumbled you, did they, sir?

MAX   (still engrossed in the photograph)   What?

PERCH   Found out your guilty secret. Rumbled the lady wife, eh? (He laughs.)

MAX   Afraid so.

(PERCH sees the wedding picture.)

PERCH   Oh, dear me, dear me! That won't do, sir. Won't do at all. Must remove all evidence of the previous incumbent.

HARRY   You sound experienced in this sort of thing.

PERCH   Only wish I was, sir. I can't get my wife to go - even for twenty-four hours! Oh, there's a gentleman downstairs, sir. Asking for you.

MAX   Didn't you tell him I had guests?

PERCH   Yes, sir, but he insisted. Says he's come to collect something that belongs to him.

MAX   This isn't the lost property office! Did he say what it was?

PERCH   Yes. His daughter.

MAX   (rising)   Oh, no!

PERCH   Says you've got 'er 'ere, sir.

HARRY   Which one?

PERCH   Sue.

HARRY   The minute that girl asked for tomato juice, I knew she'd have a father.

MAX   What's he like?

PERCH   'Ard to tell, sir. He 'asn't lost his temper, yet.

MAX	Just simmering, eh? Does he know there's a party going on?
PERCH	He knows there's something going on!
MAX	(urging him towards the door) Well, you'll have to keep him down there a little longer.
PERCH	What shall I tell him?
MAX	Tell him we're in the middle of something.
PERCH	I expect that's what he's worried about.
MAX	Just keep him out!
PERCH	Do me best. (Turning at the door.) I suppose this is what you might call a professional 'azard. (He goes out, laughing.)
	(HARRY laughs. MAX paces down to C.)
MAX	I'm glad you think it's so funny.
	(HARRY crosses to MAX D.C.)
HARRY	Just like old times. You haven't been chased by an angry father for fifteen years.
MAX	(defensively) Oh, yes, I have. I was chased by one only thirteen years ago.
HARRY	Yes, of course. I'd forgotten that. He almost caught you outside the National Provincial Bank.
MAX	Yes, but I got away!
HARRY	You could really move in those days.
MAX	I still can.
HARRY	You may have to.
MAX	What are we going to do?
HARRY	How about our old friend the fire escape? That was always a favourite.
MAX	No, no, Harry. There's a time in one's life for fire escapes, and forty-three isn't it.
HARRY	Wait a minute! What are we worried about? We have a trump card.

A BIRD IN THE HAND

MAX What?

HARRY Sylvia! A wife always lends an air of respectability.

MAX But she's not my wife any more. She's on her way out.

HARRY She can delay it. After all, it's taken twelve years to get to this stage. Another half an hour can't make any difference.

(SYLVIA comes in from R. carrying a suitcase and a parcel.)

SYLVIA We shan't be very long. Those girls are really so helpful.

(MAX and HARRY make a concerted dive to assist her, one on each side.)

HARRY Here, let me help you with that, Sylvia.

MAX You can't carry about heavy cases like that.

SYLVIA Oh, yes, I can!

HARRY We're not going to let you! (Takes her case and puts it down near the armchair.)

MAX No, certainly not!

SYLVIA What on earth's the matter with you two?

HARRY Just trying to help!

MAX Yes - that's it!

SYLVIA I know you're anxious to be rid of me, but you don't have to fall over yourselves.

HARRY Now, Sylvia, that just isn't so.

SYLVIA Isn't it?

HARRY No, of course not.

SYLVIA Well, you could have fooled me.

MAX I was just saying to Harry, 'What's her hurry, Harry?'

SYLVIA You were?

MAX Look, you come and sit down over here - (He leads her to the sofa.)

64   A BIRD IN THE HAND   Act II

HARRY   (to table D.L.)   And I'll get you a nice drink. Brandy, wasn't it?

SYLVIA What are you two up to?

MAX   We're not up to anything.

SYLVIA Five minutes ago you couldn't wait to get me out of here.

HARRY   So we've got a conscience!

SYLVIA Why, all of a sudden? You've managed without one for the last thirty years.

HARRY   Tell you what, we'll all have a nice little drink, and then later on - in about an hour, say - I'll run you to wherever you're going.

SYLVIA Now I know you're up to something!

MAX   But, Sylvia -

SYLVIA When Harry gets magnanimous you can be sure it's all to his advantage.

HARRY   (crossing to her with the brandy)   Well, you are wrong. As wrong as you can be. I am just thinking of my friend. Brandy.

SYLVIA (taking it)   Thanks.

(She looks at MAX, who assumes an air of innocence.)

So you're the one who's up to something, then?

MAX   Me? No. I just suddenly felt - sad - you know? I mean - twelve years is a long time.

SYLVIA You bet your life it's a long time, and if I don't know you now I never will.

MAX   (laying it on)   You mustn't condemn me, Sylvia, just because I'm - sentimental.

SYLVIA All of a sudden he's magnanimous and you're sentimental. You boys really must be in trouble!

(The door bell rings. The men jump like startled hares.)

What's the matter? That the night shift coming on?
(She rises.)   I'd better finish my packing.   (She gives her glass to HARRY and crosses D.R.

A BIRD IN THE HAND   65

MAX   No, Sylvia, don't go! Whoever it is - we'd like you to meet him -

SYLVIA Him?

MAX   Her! - Them! - Whoever it is!

(The door bell goes again. HARRY finishes off SYLVIA's brandy.)

SYLVIA Well, whoever it is - it's getting impatient. Thanks for the drink.   (She makes for the door R.)

HARRY   But Sylvia -

SYLVIA Maybe those boys have turned up for the party at last.

MAX   It might be for you.

SYLVIA Well, if it is, tell them I don't live here any more.
(She sweeps out.)

MAX   Now what do we do?

HARRY   I don't know about you, but I'm going down the fire escape!
(He puts down the glass and starts for the door R.)

MAX   You can't do that!

HARRY   Have they taken it away?

MAX   We'll have to go after her.

HARRY   You go. She's your wife.

MAX   But you're better at talking than me. You might talk her into it.

HARRY   It was you who talked her into it twelve years ago.

(The door bell goes yet again.)

Is that door locked?

MAX   No.

HARRY   Then what are we standing here for?   (He pulls MAX out R. quickly.)

(From the main door comes GEORGE STEVENS. He is 37 years of age, but looks a lot younger. He is neat and quick of movement and in a high state of anxiety. He marches in and is surprised to find nobody there.)

STEVENS	Oh! (He looks about, moves up to the door R., opens it and calls through.) Anybody there?	
	(Getting no reply, he paces restlessly across to D.L. and back to C.)	
	(HARRY comes in from R. He is wearing a hat. They meet C.)	
	Ah! there you are! Now, look here - !	
HARRY	(aggressively) I was told there was a party going on.	
STEVENS	Are you just arriving?	
HARRY	What does it look like? (Pointing.) That's a hat, isn't it?	
STEVENS	But the front door's out there.	
HARRY	I came up the fire escape.	
STEVENS	The fire escape?	
HARRY	(confidentially) I couldn't come in the front way. I'm not a member.	
STEVENS	But this is a private flat.	
HARRY	Then what are you doing here?	
STEVENS	You're not Max, are you?	
HARRY	No. Are you?	
STEVENS	No!	
HARRY	That makes two of us, then. (Crossing him to D.L.C.) You going to have a drink?	
STEVENS	I didn't come here to drink!	
HARRY	What did you come here for?	
STEVENS	To collect my girl.	
HARRY	You got a girl here?	
STEVENS	Yes. Her name's Sue.	
HARRY	Congratulations. I hope you'll be very happy.	
STEVENS	I'm her father!	

A BIRD IN THE HAND

HARRY	You? Come on - you couldn't be old enough.
STEVENS	(angrily) I am!
HARRY	Never. You're kidding. You're her brother. (He turns away L.)
STEVENS	(following him) I am her father!
HARRY	You're only a kid. Whatever kind of age were you when you started chasing her mother?
STEVENS	I am thirty-seven years old!
HARRY	You're not?
STEVENS	Yes, I am!
HARRY	Thirty-seven, huh? That's a good age. At that age you can still leave by the fire escape.
	(PERCH bursts in, breathless, and races down to between them.)
PERCH	You've no right barging in 'ere like that!
STEVENS	You kept me hanging about down there long enough. (Away to D.C.)
PERCH	(to HARRY) I'm sorry, sir. Did me best. He must have crept up the back stairs.
HARRY	That's all right, Perch. It doesn't matter.
PERCH	(knowingly) Everything under control, sir?
HARRY	I hope so.
PERCH	(aside) 'Idden 'em away, have you?
HARRY	Thank you, Perch. That'll be all.
PERCH	Yes, sir. You're a right one, you are. (He goes, beaming.)
	(STEVENS turns on HARRY accusingly, jabbing an accusing finger at him.)
STEVENS	He knows you! You live here! You must be the other one!
	(SUE and PEGGY come in R.)
SUE	Dad! What are you doing here?

STEVENS	Looking for you. What the hell's going on?
SUE	(to R. of STEVENS) Nothing's going on. We've had what we came here for and now we're going.
STEVENS	What did you come here for?
SUE	For dinner. Ever so nice it was, too. This is my friend Peg. This is my dad.
PEGGY	(moving in to them) Ooo - Quite young, isn't he?
HARRY	If you'll excuse me, I -
SUE	Have you met Harry?
STEVENS	Yes. We did speak.
PEGGY	Well, we're not speaking to him. Not after what he did tonight.
STEVENS	What did he do?
HARRY	I wouldn't let them watch Pinky and Perky. (He crosses below them to D.R.)
STEVENS	You said you'd just arrived.
HARRY	Yes. I lied.
STEVENS	Where are you going?
HARRY	To take my hat off. (He goes out quickly.)
SUE	Oh, Dad, you are embarrassing, coming here like this.
STEVENS	Lucky I did, by the look of it. Going out for dinner with a couple of old reprobates -
PEGGY	They're not old - they're middle-aged.
SUE	Yes. They're not much older than you are, Dad.
PEGGY	Anyhow, we weren't alone. There were two other girls.
STEVENS	You mean there were four of you?
SUE	Yes.
STEVENS	Four girls and two men?
PEGGY	Yes.
STEVENS	What are they? A couple of sex maniacs? (He circles to U.L. of the sofa.)

SUE	Oh, Dad! I thought you'd be pleased. At least we outnumbered them.
STEVENS	(grimly) Where is he? (He paces across to U.R.C.)
SUE	Who?
STEVENS	This - this Max!
SUE	He's in the bedroom.
STEVENS	What's he doing in there?
PEGGY	Talking to his wife.
	(STEVENS comes down to R. of PEGGY.)
STEVENS	(beside himself) His wife? You mean to say he's married?
SUE	Oh, yes.
STEVENS	He invited you girls here when his wife was present?
PEGGY	Yes. It's ever so respectable.
STEVENS	That's not what it sounds like to me! If I had a gun I'd shoot him!
	(SYLVIA comes in from R. with a small case. She sees STEVENS. The girls are below the R. end of the sofa.)
SYLVIA	Well, it's about time you showed up. The party's been going on for ages. Where are the rest of the boys?
STEVENS	Madam, I have come to collect my belongings!
SYLVIA	What a coincidence! So have I. Perhaps we can share a taxi.
SUE	This is my dad.
SYLVIA	Your - father?
SUE	Yes.
SYLVIA	(thoughtfully) So that's why they - I might have known.
SUE	(to STEVENS) This is Sylvia.
PEGGY	She's a wonderful cook.

A BIRD IN THE HAND — Act II

SUE — Yes - wonderful.

PEGGY — Max is her husband.

STEVENS — I should like to speak to your husband, madam!

SYLVIA — Yes, of course. And I'm sure he'll be delighted to see you. (She opens the door R. and calls.) Max! It's all right, darling. You can come in now!

(STEVENS faces the door, waiting for MAX. PEGGY and SUE exchange an apprehensive look. SYLVIA stands back, smiling, R. of the armchair.)

(MAX walks in, not immediately seeing STEVENS.)

MAX — (as he enters) Good girl! Did you get rid of the old devil?

(He freezes as he sees STEVENS. They look at each other for a moment in surprise. They obviously recognise each other. MAX goes to him.)

MAX — George!

STEVENS — Mr Winton!

MAX — I never guessed it was you.

STEVENS — No, I - I never guessed it was you, sir.

(A complete transformation has come over STEVENS. The recognition of MAX has changed him from an angry father into an apologetic underling.)

MAX — Well, this is a pleasant surprise. Not at all what I expected.

(SYLVIA drops down to D.R.)

SYLVIA — You two know each other?

MAX — You bet your life! George and I work together.

STEVENS — (modestly) Well, not exactly together, sir. (To SYLVIA.) Mr. Winton is in charge of my department. I work under him. Much lower down the ladder.

MAX — If you'd come earlier you could have joined us all for dinner.

STEVENS — That's very kind of you, Mr. Winton -

A BIRD IN THE HAND 71

MAX — Now, now! You don't have to call me Mr. Winton. Not here.

STEVENS — (the smiling sycophant) Very kind of you, sir.

MAX — Now - what are you going to have to drink?

STEVENS — Well - if you don't mind, sir - I only came to - to pick up my daughter.

MAX — Is she here?

SUE — I'm his daughter.

MAX — (to STEVENS) You're her father?

STEVENS — Yes, sir.

MAX — (nudging him playfully) Go on - you couldn't be old enough!

(STEVENS' replies are all the same as they were to HARRY, but now the anger he displayed to HARRY is replaced by a giggling sycophancy.)

STEVENS — Yes - I am, sir!

MAX — Never. You're kidding. You're her brother.

STEVENS — No, no - I'm her father! (He laughs.)

MAX — You're only a kid. You must have started pretty young.

STEVENS — (coyly) I'm thirty-seven years old!

MAX — You're not.

STEVENS — Yes - I am - honestly!

MAX — Well, I never. Thirty-seven, eh? That's about the same age as me.

SYLVIA — Huh!

MAX — Come on - let me get you a drink. (Below the girls to D.L.)

STEVENS — Well - perhaps just a small tomato juice.

MAX — Your family must have tomato juice in its veins. You don't drink much, then?

STEVENS — Only in moderation.

SYLVIA	That's how you stay looking so young.
STEVENS	That's very nice of you to say so.
SYLVIA	I mean, Max looks a lot older than you.
	(MAX gives her a look.)
PEGGY	Perhaps we'd better go and get our coats on, Sue.
SUE	Yes, okay.
	(They go to the door R.)
SYLVIA	I'll join you. You will excuse me, won't you? I'm sure you two have a lot to talk about. (She goes out with the girls.)
	(MAX brings a tomato juice and a whisky to the sofa.)
MAX	Well, come on, George - sit you down.
STEVENS	Thank you, sir. (He sits on the sofa.)
MAX	There we are - tomato juice.
STEVENS	Thanks. (He takes it.)
	(MAX sits beside him.)
MAX	Look - er - George - about this evening -
STEVENS	Oh, you don't have to explain.
MAX	Well, I wouldn't like you to misunderstand. You see, the thing is - my wife and I - we thought it would be nice to ask some of the younger people in occasionally. We thought it would broaden their outlook by having dinner and conversation with the - er - (And this hurts.) the older generation.
STEVENS	It's very kind of you, sir. I'm sure they appreciated it.
MAX	I mean, I just wouldn't like you to get the wrong impression -
STEVENS	Oh, never! Of course not, sir! Never for a moment!
MAX	That's all right, then. Cheers!
STEVENS	Cheers!

A BIRD IN THE HAND 73

(They drink.)

(HARRY peers around the door. He is astonished to see the friendly scene on the sofa.)

MAX   Oh, come on in, Harry. We're just having a drink.

HARRY   (puzzled)   Yes. So I noticed.   (He crosses to C.)

MAX   We've been having a little talk - George and I.

HARRY   George and you?

MAX   Haven't you two met?

HARRY   Well - we did exchange a few words.

STEVENS   Oh, yes. I didn't recognise you without your hat on.

HARRY   There's something different about you, too.

STEVENS   (with a laugh)   I'm sitting down.

HARRY   It could be that.

MAX   George is Sue's father.

HARRY   Go on - you couldn't be old enough!

(STEVENS reacts, temporarily finding it difficult to keep up the bonhomie, but he quickly recaptures it.)

MAX   He's come to collect her.

HARRY   That was very thoughtful of him.   (He sits beside STEVENS.)   Look - er - George, - about this evening -

MAX   Harry -

HARRY   Yes?

MAX   I did all that.

HARRY   Oh - fine!

STEVENS   (rising to D.L. of the sofa)   Well, I'd better be on my way. I'm sorry I interrupted your evening.

MAX   (rising to R. of STEVENS)   That's quite all right, George. Think nothing of it.

HARRY   Yes - come again another time.

STEVENS	Thank you for the drink, sir.	

(HARRY reacts to the 'sir' and looks enquiringly at MAX, who shrugs benignly.)

MAX George works in my office.

(HARRY rises and turns away to L. of the armchair to hide his enjoyment of this.)

STEVENS Well, goodbye, sir. See you in the morning.   (He moves upstage towards the door.)

MAX (following to L. of STEVENS)   Aren't you forgetting something?

STEVENS H'm?

MAX Your daughter.

STEVENS Oh, that's all right. I don't want to spoil your evening.

MAX (firmly)   The evening is over, George.

STEVENS Well, if you're sure you've finished with her -

(HARRY and MAX exchange a look as SUE and PEGGY come in, wearing their coats. They walk past HARRY without looking at him, and go up to where STEVENS is waiting.)

SUE All right, Dad. We're ready.

(The girls start to go out.)

STEVENS Just a minute!

(The girls stop in the doorway.)

Have you both forgotten your manners?   (Indicating the men.)   Say thank you for having me.

(But this only strikes the girls as highly amusing, and they go out of the door in fits of giggles. STEVENS looks helplessly at MAX and HARRY, shrugs, giggles nervously and follows the girls out, closing the door behind him. MAX and HARRY both laugh. MAX crosses down to U.L. of the sofa.)

MAX How do you like that? I think he'd sell his own grandmother for promotion!

A BIRD IN THE HAND

(They are laughing as SYLVIA comes in R. She is ready to go. She picks up her suitcase, etc., and makes for the door L.)

SYLVIA (brightly) Well - I'm the next!

(MAX intercepts her U.C.)

MAX Sylvia -

SYLVIA Yes?

MAX You - you going somewhere?

SYLVIA I'm leaving you, Max. Had you forgotten?

MAX What - now? I mean, it's a bit late to find -

SYLVIA I'll manage. Well, you did ask me to go.

MAX Yes, I know, but -

SYLVIA And you were right. As long as I know Harry's here to look after you I'm quite happy. (She crosses above him to the steps.)

MAX (following to her R.) Are you - er - going to leave a forwarding address?

SYLVIA I'll let you know where I end up. Goodbye, Harry.

HARRY So long, Sylvia. Drop in again some time.

(SYLVIA and MAX look at each other for a moment.)

SYLVIA Goodbye, Max.

MAX Goodbye, Sylvia -

(She leans forward and kisses him lightly on the cheek. She turns to go, then remembers something.)

SYLVIA I almost forgot.

(She takes the latchkey out of her pocket and holds it out to MAX.)

You'd better have this. I wouldn't want you to have to change the lock.

(A tiny pause, then he takes the key. She smiles, picks up her case and goes out.)

(MAX, in a bit of a daze, moves down to below the sofa and sits, still holding the key. HARRY attempts to break the sudden atmosphere. He moves in to R. of the sofa.)

HARRY Well, Max - back to the old days, huh? Just you and me - and the girls! We are going to have a ball!

MAX (dully)   Yes -

(HARRY sits beside him on the sofa.)

HARRY What's the matter?

MAX You know something, Harry -

HARRY What?

MAX I think she's gone for good -

(HARRY turns and looks at him, aware of a pinpoint of regret.)

(At that moment the door R. bursts open and MISS FERGUSON comes in. She is wearing an apron. The men react and rise.)

HARRY Miss Ferguson! We'd forgotten all about you!

MAX Have you been out the back - typing away - all this time?

HARRY You should have gone with Sylvia.

MAX I'll go and stop her -   (He rises.)

GRETA No - there's no need! I'm not going.

(HARRY rises slowly in horror.)

HARRY You're - not - going?

GRETA No. Sylvia insisted and I promised.

MAX (ominously)   Promised what?

GRETA That I'd stay here and look after you boys. Sylvia couldn't bear the thought of you cooking for yourselves.

HARRY But, Miss Ferguson, we don't need -

GRETA It's all settled. I've made up a bed for you in the spare room.

HARRY	(ungraciously) Thanks.
GRETA	I'll be up first thing in the morning to cook your breakfast. And now, if you don't mind, I'm going to get some sleep. Goodnight!
	(She starts to go, then stops.)
	Oh, there is just one thing.
HARRY	Yes?
GRETA	How do you like your kipper fillets?
	(MAX and HARRY react apprehensively and sink onto the sofa in unison.)

CURTAIN

ACT THREE

The following evening. It is getting dark outside, but the curtains are not yet drawn and the electric lights are not on.

MAX is slumped in the armchair, gazing into space. HARRY comes in from outside, his step lively, carrying a briefcase. He does not at first see MAX. Humming a little tune, he throws his hat onto a chair, puts down his briefcase on the sofa table, takes off his jacket, loosens his tie, moves down C. and sees MAX.

HARRY   Oh, hullo, Max.   (He continues below the sofa, but getting no response he returns.)   Max -

MAX   (vaguely)   Oh - hullo -   (He waves a paw.) You're back early.

HARRY   (glancing at his watch)   What are you talking about? It's after six-thirty.

MAX   You mean to say the sun has gone?

HARRY   Almost. What are you doing sitting here in the dark? (He goes and switches on the lights.)

A BIRD IN THE HAND

(MAX utters a cry and covers his eyes.)

MAX Aaah! Turn it off!

(HARRY turns it off. He comes down and looks at MAX.)

HARRY Okay, Max - what time did you start drinking?

MAX What time did we stop?

HARRY One o'clock when we went to bed.

MAX Then I started again at nine o'clock when you went to work.

HARRY But that's terrible. All I've had all day is a cold beer at lunchtime.

MAX Yes. But you've been at the office.

HARRY Well, haven't you?

MAX (shaking his head sombrely)   Today just had to be one of the times I work at home.

HARRY And so?

MAX Have you ever tried working in the middle of a power station? Because that's what it's been like here today.

HARRY Look, Max - we can't sit here in the dark. I'm turning the lights on - okay?

MAX (reluctantly)   Okay. But - do it gently.

(MAX closes his eyes and HARRY turns the lights on. Slowly MAX opens his eyes, blinking as he gets used to it. HARRY returns to him.)

HARRY My God, you look awful! So this is what happens when you're left alone?

MAX I wasn't alone. Miss Ferguson has been here. Miss Ferguson has been here - all day!

HARRY Don't tell me little Miss Ferguson made the place seem like a power station? She's only a girl.

MAX That's what you think. When she hasn't been clacking away on her typewriter, she has been cleaning, and scrubbing - and playing the washing-up machine! I've never known anyone get such a terrible sound out of a washing-up

	machine. And as for the hoover! I think she must have had it amplified.
HARRY	That the only reason you've been drinking?
MAX	What?
HARRY	Because of Miss Ferguson?
	(MAX lowers his eyes.)
MAX	What - er - what other reason could there be?
HARRY	(with a smile) I just wondered. (He moves below the sofa, looking about.) Anyhow, we've got a nice clean flat. Looks great.
MAX	Harry, before Miss Ferguson started tidying I could only find half my things. Now I can't find anything!
HARRY	Where is she now?
MAX	She finally switched everything off at five o'clock and went for a walk in the park.
HARRY	Well, you'd better get yourself a shower and freshen up a little, because we're in for a big evening.
	(MAX blinks half-heartedly.)
MAX	We are?
HARRY	You bet. Look what I picked up today. (He goes to MAX and takes out a red note book.) I went over to my place at lunchtime. Remember that?
	(MAX peers at it.)
MAX	What is it? The Old Testament?
HARRY	The Old Testament is the only book with more names in it than this! And these are all girls.
MAX	(smiling bleakly) I remember now. You had a red one and I had a blue one. We were really organised in those days.
HARRY	Whatever happened to yours?
MAX	Sylvia sent it to the W.V.S. along with the jumble.

A BIRD IN THE HAND 81

HARRY (generously) You can share mine.

MAX Thanks, Harry.

HARRY And I tell you this - I've been keeping mine up to date. We'll pick out a few of the really good ones - and lift the phone!

MAX And then?

HARRY When they hear you and I are back in business they'll come running.

MAX (suddenly feeling rather ill) I don't feel like it.

HARRY You will, Max. When they get here you'll feel great.

MAX (miserably) I feel sick.

(HARRY pulls MAX to his feet.)

HARRY (urging him to the door) Have a cold shower, take an alka-seltzer, put on a clean shirt and you'll feel a new man.

MAX I can still feel that egg that Miss Ferguson cooked for breakfast. You'd think boiling an egg was easy, wouldn't you?

HARRY Not to her. She must be the only woman I know who has a timer set for a ten-minute egg.

MAX You know I bent my spoon trying to get the top off?

HARRY Take the tablet and forget it!

MAX (turning back with sudden fear) What are we going to do about food tonight? If Miss Ferguson has difficulty coping with breakfast, just think what she could do to a major meal.

HARRY We'll go out and eat. There's a Chinese restaurant just around the corner.

MAX (shuddering) Don't remind me!

HARRY Oh. Oh, yes. I'd forgotten. We'll go somewhere else. But - no curry, eh? Something more easy to digest. (He taps his stomach ruefully.)

MAX We could always send out for some tins of baby food.

HARRY	Very funny. Take a shower.
MAX	(in the doorway) You know something, Harry?
HARRY	What?
MAX	Today has been even worse than being married. (He goes out.)
	(HARRY reacts to MAX's remark and then, determined not to let MAX depress him, trips lightly across towards the drinks table.)
	(PERCH comes in with a box containing some bottles.)
PERCH	Reinforcements, sir!
HARRY	Ah, good man. Put 'em over here, will you?
PERCH	Right, sir. (He goes to the drinks table to unload.) I'll never 'ave the nerve to go into that shop and just ask for a bottle of brown ale after this. (Confidentially.) She - she went, then, sir?
HARRY	Last night.
PERCH	Wonder how long he'll stay liberated this time.
HARRY	Depends whether he enjoys his freedom. Takes a bit of getting used to, y'know.
PERCH	(with great longing) I'd like to 'ave the chance, sir.
HARRY	Put that beer in the fridge, will you?
PERCH	Right you are. (He picks up the beer and makes for the door R.) I suppose you two'll be getting into your stride now, eh?
HARRY	That's the idea.
PERCH	(turning at the doorway) You - er - you got some stuff coming in tonight, 'ave you?
HARRY	We will have.
PERCH	You mean you 'aven't even lined it up yet?
HARRY	(blithely) There's the telephone!
PERCH	(speechless with admiration) Blimey! You two must 'ave been a couple of buggers when you were young! (He goes out with the beer.)

A BIRD IN THE HAND

(HARRY reacts to the word 'young', but shrugs it off.)

(GRETA FERGUSON comes in from the main door, rather breathless, carrying her handbag and a basket of shopping, and crosses to R. of the sofa.)

GRETA   I expect you were wondering what had happened to me.

HARRY   No, Miss Ferguson. Just hoping.

GRETA   I came back as quickly as I could.

HARRY   There was no need to hurry.

GRETA   I said to the man in the supermarket, 'I've got to be quick so I can get back and feed my boys'. (She puts her coat down on the armchair.)

HARRY   (cringeing) Why'd you go to the supermarket?

GRETA   There was nothing in for dinner.

HARRY   Oh, we won't be in for dinner. We'll go out to eat.

GRETA   There's no need to do that. I've got everything here. The man in the supermarket gave me a recipe. It's for a sort of casserole. It can't be too difficult. I'm sure I'll be able to manage it - with a bit of luck.

HARRY   (to L. of the sofa) No, really, I -

GRETA   But it sounds delicious!

HARRY   Yes, I'm sure it sounds lovely, but we wouldn't dream of taking up your time. I'm sure you have a lot of typing to do.

GRETA   That's all right. I can do that while you're having your dessert. (She goes to the door R.)

(PERCH returns. He is somewhat taken aback to see MISS FERGUSON.)

PERCH   And what are you doing 'ere?

GRETA   Waiting for you to hold the door.

(PERCH, put off-balance by her counter attack, mutters and holds the door for her. She goes through blithely.)

Thank you. (Exit.)

PERCH   How long's she staying for?

HARRY   I don't know. But I have my fears. Oh, Perch, I wonder if you'd pop out and get me some more cigarettes?
(He takes out some money.)

PERCH   Right you are, sir.   (He takes the money and heads for the door.)   You want me to get rid of her, sir?

HARRY   Could you?

PERCH   You leave it to me!   (He winks and goes out.)

MAX   (off R.)   Harry!

HARRY   Yes?

MAX   (off)   Where'd you put the alka-seltzer?

HARRY   Don't ask me. You're the one who lives here.

(MAX comes in, wearing a bathrobe, his hair awry.)

MAX   It is not in the bathroom cupboard!

HARRY   I never said it was.

MAX   That's where it lives.

HARRY   Well, I never touched it.

MAX   You had it for breakfast this morning. You sat there smiling over it while I was wrestling with my egg.

HARRY   I did? Then it must be with the marmalade. Kitchen cupboard. Top shelf.

MAX   Thanks.   (He starts to go.)

HARRY   Feeling better?

MAX   Yes. Who knows? I may even live.

HARRY   Good. I'll start ringing around.

MAX   What?

HARRY   (holding it up)   The little red book.

MAX   (doubtfully)   Oh - er - yes.

HARRY   Oh, come on! After alka-seltzer and a whisky chaser you'll feel like a new man.

MAX	Oh. I thought you were talking about girls. (He goes out R.)
	(HARRY laughs, settles himself on the sofa with his drink and pulls the telephone nearer. He looks through the red book, finds a number and dials. While the number is ringing he takes a sip of whisky and settles down optimistically in a chair.)
HARRY	Hullo? Is that 4285? Fine! Could I speak to Nancy Clarke, please? What? What d'you mean she won't speak to me? She doesn't know who it is. She did what? You sure of that? No, no, I suppose you wouldn't make a mistake about a thing like that. Okay. Never mind. If you happen to see her - just say Harry phoned. No, I don't expect it would make any difference, no. Okay. Goodbye. (He hangs up, disconsolately, and crosses the name out in his red book.)
	(MAX comes in, carrying a bubbling glass of alka-seltzer. He moves to R. of the sofa.)
MAX	You know, Harry, I knew a man once who got hooked on alka-seltzer. You know what happened? His wife woke up one day and found he'd gone with the wind! (He laughs delightedly at his terrible joke. Then he realises that HARRY isn't laughing, shrugs and drinks the alka-seltzer. He shudders, races to the drinks table and grabs a whisky. He sips it gratefully.)
	What's the matter? You usually laugh at my awful jokes.
HARRY	(gloomily) I just phoned Nancy Clarke.
MAX	Oh, great! Is she coming round?
HARRY	She can't.
MAX	Why not?
HARRY	She's living in a convent.
MAX	A what?
HARRY	A convent, for Christ's sake!
MAX	Nancy Clarke?

HARRY	Yes.	
MAX	You mean she's a nun?	
HARRY	Who else lives in a convent?	
MAX	But - Nancy Clarke! She was fond of a good time.	
HARRY	Yes. (With admiration.) That girl must have spent half her life in the confessional.	
MAX	So maybe she decided it was easier to join.	

(The telephone rings. Automatically HARRY lifts the receiver. MAX looks hopeful and moves in to L. of the sofa.)

HARRY	Yes? Oh - yes. Just a minute.
MAX	For me?
HARRY	You expecting a call?
MAX	Well, I - I thought perhaps Sylvia - She said she'd let me have a forwarding address.
HARRY	It's for Miss Ferguson.
MAX	(disappointed) Oh. Right. I'll call her. Miss Fergus - ! (He stops and holds his head in agony.) Ooh. You call her.
HARRY	(calling) Miss Ferguson!

(GRETA comes in immediately.)

GRETA	There's no need to shout.
HARRY	What were you doing? Listening at the keyhole? It's for you.
GRETA	The telephone?
HARRY	Yes.
GRETA	For me?
HARRY	Yes.
GRETA	But nobody knows I'm -
MAX	(painfully) Will you answer the phone!

A BIRD IN THE HAND   87

GRETA   You shouldn't drink so much, then you wouldn't have a bad head.

MAX   Thank you, Miss Ferguson. I'll try to remember.

GRETA   (taking the receiver from HARRY)   Hullo? Yes - speaking. Oh - really? But she never said that when I - Oh, I see. All right. I'll be there. Thank you.   (She hangs up.)   Oh, dear. I'm afraid I'll have to leave you.

HARRY   (in mock anguish)   Oh, Miss Ferguson - no!

GRETA   I've no alternative. Duty calls.

HARRY   Well, I suppose we'll manage somehow.

GRETA   (getting her handbag from the sofa table)   I shan't be able to cook that meal for you now.

HARRY   No, you won't, will you? What a shame!

GRETA   Of course, I suppose I could always -

         (HARRY rises quickly to her R.)

HARRY   (quickly)   That's okay - we'll go out to eat!   (He helps her into her coat.)

GRETA   Are you sure you'll be all right?

MAX   (quickly to her L.)   Yes - fine! Fine!

GRETA   Oh, dear - I've left the food out on the table - I'd better just go and -

HARRY   We'll see to it!   (He collects her hat from the sofa table and they urge her towards the door.)

GRETA   I don't really like letting you down -

MAX   You're not doing that!

GRETA   Well, if you're sure you can manage -

HARRY   Don't you worry!

GRETA   I'll let myself in quietly. After last night I expect you'll want to get to bed early.

HARRY   Goodnight, Miss Ferguson!   (He plonks her hat down

88 A BIRD IN THE HAND Act III

on her head at a rakish angle. They urge her out and shut the door after her.)

MAX That's a relief!

HARRY Yes. Good old Perch! (Moving back to the sofa.) Okay, Max, let's get down to business. Who'll we try next? Let's see now - (He sits and thumbs through the address book.)

(MAX wanders down to R. of the sofa.)

MAX (thoughtfully) How about Betty Delaware?

HARRY Is that another of your jokes?

MAX No. I mean it.

HARRY But that's going back a long way.

MAX She was a nice girl.

HARRY She was a big girl. Stood about seventeen hands high.

MAX Yes? I only remember her sitting down.

HARRY Sitting down she was still tall.

(MAX sits beside HARRY.)

MAX Nice girl, though. Lovely eyes. Blue. I used to see a lot of Betty at one time.

HARRY You couldn't help seeing a lot of Betty at one time! Here - what about Jackie Brewer?

MAX She had a good family.

HARRY Never mind the family. What about the girl?

MAX (not too keen) She was always talking about 'Mummy' and 'Daddy' and Harrods. She was so smart I bet you had to wear a dinner jacket to kiss her goodnight.

HARRY Come to think of it, she was a bit on the cool side.

MAX That's no surprise. Her father ran a frozen fish finger factory.

HARRY Maybe we'd better forget her. She'll have married a merchant banker by now, anyway. Here we are! This is the one! Janet - Marshall!

A BIRD IN THE HAND

MAX   (blankly)   Who?

HARRY   What's the matter with you? You must remember Janet Marshall! She worked in a biscuit factory.

MAX   Did she eat them in bed?

HARRY   Another of your jokes. I used to take her out dancing and she brought along a friend for you.

MAX   (ominously)   Oh, yes. The friend I remember. She was an eager girl with a dental problem.

HARRY   So shall I call Janet?

MAX   (without enthusiasm)   Yes - okay - if you like.

HARRY   (as he dials)   Oh, come on - cheer up! Maybe she's got better friends these days. Anyhow, I never noticed you trying to get away from that girl.

MAX   I was afraid she might have bitten me. She had incisors like Count Dracula.

HARRY   (into the phone)   Hullo. Does Janet Marshall still live there, please? She does? It is? Oh, great.
(He winks at MAX.)   Hullo, Janet. This is Harry.
(Pause.)   What d'you mean 'Harry who'? Harry Tyler! Yes, I know it's a long time. Well, I've been rather busy lately. As long as that, eh?   (He laughs.)
Look, Max and I thought it would be - What? Max - Max Winton - you remember him. Yes, that's the one!
(He laughs at what she has said.)

MAX   (angrily)   What is she saying?

HARRY   She says she remembers you.   (He is still chuckling.)

MAX   What did she say about me?

(HARRY indicates to MAX to keep quiet.)

HARRY   (into 'phone)   Yes. We thought it would be nice if you popped over and had a drink - you know? For old time's sake. You will? Great!   (He gives the 'thumbs up' to MAX.)   What? Oh. Well - actually, Janet - we - er - Well, no, we don't really need any more men. No. Well, no, I suppose he wouldn't understand that. Well, maybe some other time, then. Okay, Janet. Nice talking to you.   (He hangs up, despondently.)

A BIRD IN THE HAND — Act III

MAX Maybe we'd better just forget the whole thing.

HARRY What do you mean?

MAX We've been out of action for so long, Harry. You can't expect all these girls still to be waiting for us.

HARRY Why not?

MAX They'll all be married and settled down and bringing up families by now. They won't be sitting by the telephone wondering why we never call them.

HARRY Now you're being defeatist again! I tell you, Max, there's some vintage wine in this book. All right, so we left it standing for a while - but the good wine will be all the better for it!

MAX All we'll find will be empty bottles.

HARRY All right, then, so we'll concentrate on the younger girls.

MAX The younger girls will be concentrating on the younger men.

HARRY (the eternal optimist) There's plenty to go around! They're producing more every day. Anyhow, I tell you, they prefer older men.

MAX Like those two last night? You heard all those remarks about my age? They thought we were a couple of dirty old men!

HARRY No, they did not! I tell you, we're in our prime.

MAX Yes - you know that, and I know that - but they don't know that. They think we were in our prime when they were in their prams.

(The phone rings.)

HARRY (his heart lifting) What'll you bet she's changed her mind and ditched the boy-friend? (He picks up the receiver.) Changed your mind, eh? No, it isn't. This is Harry Tyler. Helen? I don't believe it! It's great to hear from you! (To MAX.) It's Helen.

(MAX looks blank.)

Well, how have you been all this time? Yes - he's right here. (To MAX.) Say hello to Helen.

A BIRD IN THE HAND

MAX   (into phone)   Hullo, Helen.

HARRY   (immediately bringing the receiver back to himself) Funny you should ring. Max and I were just sitting here, having a drink, and I said to Max, 'Why don't we call Helen?' Yes! And right away you rang! It's uncanny. What? She isn't! Right there with you? Fantastic! (To MAX.)   Frances is there, too.   (He holds out the receiver.)

MAX   (into phone)   Hullo, Frances.

HARRY   (once again taking back the receiver)   Well, this is incredible. What? No, this is Harry. That was Max. Yes, the one who said 'Hullo, Frances'. Look - where are you girls speaking from? But that's just around the corner. Why don't you grab a taxi and come right around? It'll be like the old days. A few drinks and go out to dinner. What do you say? Wonderful! Flat 24, Grantham Towers. See you.   (He hangs up.)   Max, we are in business! Didn't I tell you? The word has got around! (He takes MAX's glass and goes to replenish their drinks.)

MAX   Helen and Frances, eh? We certainly had some great times with those girls.

HARRY   You know, I thought at one time you might have married Frances.

MAX   (smiling coyly)   Well, I won't say I never thought about it!

HARRY   Maybe I should have married Helen. Maybe it would all have worked out - Oh, what the hell! We're all still here, that's the main thing.   (He hands a fresh drink to MAX.)   Well - here's to it, Max. The old days!

MAX   The old days -

(They clink glasses and drink solemnly.)

HARRY   Here, you'd better go and get some trousers on. You can't greet a couple of girls looking like that.

(MAX rises.)

MAX   Oh - yes! Might give them the wrong idea, eh?   (He crosses R.)

HARRY	You'd better hurry it up, too. They only have to come around the corner.	
MAX	Funny, that. All this time Helen's been living just around the corner - and we never knew.	
HARRY	We know now.	
MAX	Yes. (He goes out R.)	

(PERCH taps on the door and comes in with the cigarettes to R. of the sofa.)

PERCH	The cigarettes, sir.
HARRY	Oh, thank you, Perch. (He takes them.) No, you keep the change. I think you've earned it.
PERCH	Oh - thank you very much, sir. (He pockets the change gratefully.) You got anything fixed up yet, sir?
HARRY	We certainly have.
PERCH	You didn't waste much time, did you?
HARRY	Mustn't let the grass grow.

(During the next bit of dialogue, HARRY draws the curtains, turns on various lamps, and turns off the main lights to provide a better atmosphere. PERCH watches, approvingly.)

PERCH	What are they like?
HARRY	Really something! I think you'll approve, Perch.
PERCH	Same sort of thing as last night, sir?
HARRY	Oh, no! These two have got class.
PERCH	Well, I thought the other two were quite pretty, sir. No complaint about them.
HARRY	You wait till you see this lot.
PERCH	I don't know how you do it, sir. I can't even get my wife to go, never mind find meself a bird.

(HARRY takes out an aerosol spray from his briefcase and sprays the room. PERCH gazes in awe.)

	What's that, sir?
HARRY	Chanel Number Five.
PERCH	Blimey!
HARRY	Now let's have a little music - (He turns on the record player. A romantic tune.) There we are, Perch. How's that?
PERCH	What I'd give for a pad like this. (He makes for the door.)
HARRY	Leave the door ajar, will you? The young ladies will be here in a minute, so show them up, won't you? They don't know the way.
PERCH	Reckon they'll find it if they follow their noses, sir.
	(PERCH goes out. MAX returns, having dressed. He reacts to the perfume.)
MAX	What the hell have you been doing? Let's get some fresh air. (He makes for the window.)
	(HARRY intercepts him.)
HARRY	You leave that window alone!
MAX	But it's like a chemist's shop in here.
HARRY	That is Chanel Number Five and it cost me a fortune. I will not have it wasted on the night air.
MAX	Harry, we never needed perfume sprays in the old days! You might at least have used the air freshener.
HARRY	If you hadn't filled the place with kipper fillets I wouldn't have had to use anything!
MAX	All right. Let's just hope it'll drift a little before they get here. Well - how do I look?
HARRY	(without enthusiasm) I suppose you'll be okay if we keep the lights down. You decided not to wear the Crown Topper, then?
MAX	Ha, ha. Very funny. How about you, anyway? Every time you move I can hear your corsets squeak.

	(They both laugh.)
HARRY	What are we doing standing here with two empty glasses? We must be losing our touch. (He takes the glasses to be refilled.)
	(MAX drops down to C.)
MAX	There was no call, was there? When I was in the shower.
HARRY	Call? Who from?
MAX	Er - from Sylvia.
HARRY	Sylvia? Who's she?
MAX	You know - my - er -
HARRY	Oh, yes - Sylvia - that was her name.
MAX	I - I just thought she might have called - you know. (Embarrassed, he turns away to L. of the armchair.)
	(HARRY brings the drinks to MAX.)
HARRY	Once and for all, Max, - will you forget about Sylvia? It's all over - kaput - finished!
MAX	I just thought she might have called. That's all.
	(The door-bell rings.)
HARRY	There they are! The girls are here! (Calling.) Come on in, girls! The door's open! (To MAX.) Do me a favour, Max. Let's try to forget about Sylvia - just for tonight?
MAX	(with a smile) Okay. She's forgotten.
HARRY	Great! (He moves below the sofa to D.L.) Come on, girls! We're in here waiting for you!

(The door opens and the girls come in. HELEN and FRANCES are no longer what they used to be. They have obviously been pretty, but time has not treated them as kindly as it might have done. HELEN is plump, jolly with dyed blonde hair; FRANCES, the quieter of the two, is still attractive though definitely faded. They are both in their mid-forties. They are hardly what we - or the men - expected, but it is important that HELEN and

A BIRD IN THE HAND

        FRANCES are not caricatures and they must be slightly pathetic as well as funny. They move down between the men.)

HELEN   Harry!

FRANCES   Max!

        (They move in on the men and embrace them heartily. MAX and HARRY, over the girls' shoulders, look at each other in horror.)

HELEN   How wonderful to see you boys again!

HARRY   (trying hard)   Great to see you, Frances.

HELEN   I'm not Frances. She's Frances.

HARRY   Yes, of course! You think I didn't know that?   (He tries to laugh off his error.)

HELEN   Ah! you naughty old thing! You were just kidding, eh? Same old Harry!   (She laughs and cuddles him a little.)

FRANCES   Hullo, Max.

MAX   Frances -   (Rather too firmly.)   You haven't changed a bit.

FRANCES   (with a smile)   Not after fifteen years?

MAX   Is it as long as that?

FRANCES   You still look the same.

MAX   I looked middle-aged when I was born.

        (MAX lowers his eyes, slightly embarrassed by the rapport that still exists between them. PERCH looks in.)

PERCH   No sign of 'em yet, sir!   (He sees the girls.) Oh, beg your pardon.   (He backs out, reacting unfavourably to tonight's batch.)

HELEN   I wouldn't have been surprised if you hadn't recognised me, Harry. I mean - after all - I must have put on a few pounds since you last saw me!

HARRY   Well - er - maybe just a few, huh?   (He laughs nervously.)

HELEN   What kind of a waist did I have in those days?

HARRY   Great - just great!

HELEN   24? 25, maybe?

HARRY   About that.

HELEN   You try getting an arm around me now!

           (They all laugh, but it dies.)

HARRY   Well, come and sit down, girls. How about a drink?

           (MAX takes their coats and puts them down on a chair upstage. HELEN and FRANCES sit on the sofa. HARRY goes to the drinks. MAX hovers R. of the sofa.)

HELEN   Gin, please, Harry. And don't tell me it's fattening. I know all that. But I passed the point of no return long ago.

HARRY   How about you, Frances?

FRANCES   Have you got a glass of wine?

HARRY   Beaujolais?

FRANCES   Fine.

           (HARRY pours the drinks.)

MAX   You always used to drink brandy in the old days.

           (FRANCES looks at him, quite touched that he should remember.)

FRANCES   (warmly)   Oh, you remembered. You're a nice man.

MAX   Brandy and dry ginger.

FRANCES   I gave it up. I found it made me melancholy.

HELEN   I thought you gave it up because you had an ulcer.

FRANCES   Who asked you?

MAX   It was funny you ringing up like that - out of the blue.

FRANCES   Well, we got talking -

HELEN   You know how we girls are!

FRANCES   Thinking about the old days - you know - and we suddenly thought how nice it would be to see you both again.

A BIRD IN THE HAND

HELEN   So we looked you up in the phone book and here we are!

HARRY   (arriving with the drinks)   Gin for you, Helen.

HELEN   Thanks.

HARRY   And wine for you.

FRANCES   Thanks, Harry.

(They take their drinks.)

HARRY   You still going, Max?

MAX   Yes. I'm fine.

HARRY   Well - here's to - what shall we say?

HELEN   I know! Here's to - being together again.

(HARRY and MAX exchange an apprehensive look.)

HARRY   Er - yes - being together again.

HELEN   (coyly)   And may it be for a long time.

(The girls smile at each other and drink. The men hesitate for a second, then follow suit.)

HELEN   You're not married, then, Harry?

HARRY   No! Er - no. Not any more.

FRANCES   You have been, then?

HARRY   I tried it for a little while.

HELEN   I knew someone would get you in the end.

FRANCES   What happened? You find a girl who could run faster than you?

MAX   He's been married three times.

FRANCES   You have?

HARRY   Can't you tell? Just count the rings around my eyes.

HELEN   Three times, eh?   (She holds out her hand.)
Well - shake!

HARRY   What?

HELEN   Same here.

HARRY	You?
HELEN	I just got rid of my third. (She laughs.)
HARRY	Oh - I'm sorry.
HELEN	No need to be sorry. He was more upset than I was.
FRANCES	Yes. He was quite sad when they parted.
HELEN	He'll be sadder still when he has to pay the maintenance!
HARRY	Yes. I know how it feels.
HELEN	So - I'm not starving. But I am alone, Harry. (She giggles coyly.)
HARRY	Oh - er - yes. (He escapes quickly to replenish his glass.)
MAX	You married, Frances?
FRANCES	Not any more.
MAX	(trying to keep it gay) What kind of a score did you knock up?
FRANCES	Only one.
MAX	Oh.
HELEN	Well, at least you broke your duck! (She pushes FRANCES playfully.)
MAX	What happened to him?
FRANCES	He walked out on me.
HELEN	He went off with a girl of nineteen! How about that? Dirty old man.
MAX	Perhaps I will have another drink, Harry. (He crosses to HARRY to get a refill.)
HELEN	At least she got a lot of money out of him. He was very generous in that way, wasn't he, Frances?
FRANCES	Oh, yes. And how about you, Max?
MAX	What's that?
HELEN	You're the only one who hasn't come out in the open. What's your score?

A BIRD IN THE HAND 99

MAX	Just one.
HELEN	Divorced?
MAX	Not yet.
HELEN	Still pending, eh?
MAX	Something like that. (Embarrassed, he moves away above the sofa to U.C.)
HELEN	So we're all in the same boat! All married and all divorced - or will be, soon. Lucky thing we all met up.
MAX	Yes -

(A short pause, then FRANCES comes to the rescue. She rises and moves D.R., looking about.)

FRANCES Nice place you got here, Max.

(MAX comes down to L. of her.)

MAX You like it?

FRANCES I think it's charming.

MAX That's Sylvia. She's very good at picking colours - you know.

FRANCES Sylvia?

MAX Yes. My - er - my - er -   (He can't say the word in front of them.)

FRANCES Oh - yes. Looks like she had good taste.

MAX (trying to make a joke)   Except when she picked me, huh?   (He laughs unnaturally.)

FRANCES The mistake she made was letting you go.

HELEN I always said you should have grabbed Max when you had the chance.

FRANCES How could I ? He was almost as quick a runner as Harry.

HELEN Never too late. Better try again now he's slowed down a little!

(They all laugh, but it is a bit of a strain for MAX and HARRY. MAX tries to break the atmosphere - and change the subject - by moving up to the record player.)

MAX	Let's have some more music, shall we?
HELEN	Well, you boys haven't lost your touch. You still know how to set it up.
HARRY	What d'you mean?
HELEN	Well - shaded lights, plenty to drink, music playing - and what the hell have you been spraying the room with?
HARRY	I can't smell anything! Can you, Max?
MAX	No! No, not a thing! You want me to open a window?
HELEN	No. I'm not complaining. I love it. It gets me in the mood.
	(MAX hastily starts the music. A slow waltz, vintage early 50's. FRANCES reacts to it and moves U.R. towards the window.)
FRANCES	Oh, Max - you even picked the music.
MAX	(alarmed) I did?
FRANCES	This tune!
MAX	You like it?
FRANCES	I certainly do.
MAX	I'll turn it off -
FRANCES	No! It's one of my favourites.
HELEN	(rising decisively) You know something? All of a sudden I feel like dancing. (She joins FRANCES.) Be just like the old days, won't it, Frances?
HARRY	(aside) Oh, my God! (He hastily refills his glass.)
FRANCES	You still like dancing, Max? I remember you were quite a maestro.
MAX	That's a long time ago. I couldn't remember the steps now.
FRANCES	Oh, come on - don't be an old spoilsport!
HELEN	You were pretty good, too, Harry - in the old days.
HARRY	Well, I've got this tricky tendon in my ankle -

A BIRD IN THE HAND 101

HELEN	(to FRANCES) You remember Harry's quickstep, don't you? He could have won a prize if he'd wanted to.
	(HELEN and FRANCES talk to each other upstage.)
	(MAX joins HARRY at the drinks table and gratefully accepts a refill. They speak quietly.)
HARRY	Oh, brother! We'll have to get them out of here.
MAX	Yes. I - I suppose we will.
HARRY	And I thought we were in luck! Leave it to me. I'll think of something.
	(HELEN and FRANCES move down in unison. FRANCES pulls MAX to U.R. HELEN grabs HARRY and prepares to dance D.L.)
HELEN	Okay, boys - let's go!
MAX	It's no good, Frances - I can't remember -
FRANCES	You'll pick it up again in no time -
HARRY	I never was any good at the waltz, I tell you -
HELEN	Of course you were - you're just being modest -
FRANCES	It's simple - just count one, two, three - it'll soon come back -
HELEN	One, two, three - okay, Harry?
FRANCES) HELEN)	(together) One, two, three - one, two, three - one, two, three -
	(The girls continue counting out the time, and the men stumble uncertainly into a waltz, muttering protestations the while. As they do so, the door opens and SYLVIA and GRETA sail in. They stop on the steps and view the spectacle in amused surprise. At last the men see them and break away from their partners, HARRY to D.L., MAX to R. of the armchair. HELEN and FRANCES see SYLVIA and GRETA who come down to above the sofa. HARRY turns off the music and drops D.L. again.
MAX	(weakly) Hullo, Sylvia -
SYLVIA	Well, you boys have turned into a couple of little Fred Astaires, haven't you?

102   A BIRD IN THE HAND   Act III

MAX	This is quite a surprise -
HELEN	Aren't you going to introduce us?
MAX	Oh, yes. This is - er -
SYLVIA	Sylvia.
MAX	Yes, that's right - Sylvia.
HELEN	We know what she's called, but what does she do?
MAX	She's - she's my wife.
HELEN	Oh, so you're the one who's 'pending' !
SYLVIA	I beg your pardon?
MAX	(quickly) This is Helen - and Frances.
SYLVIA	How do you do. This is my secretary, Greta Ferguson.
HELEN	Hullo, there.
GRETA	How do you do.
SYLVIA	Poor Miss Ferguson was going all the way over to my office on a wild goose chase. Somebody must have given her the wrong information. Wasn't that unkind?
HARRY	You mean that phone call was a hoax?
GRETA	Looks like it.
HARRY	Now, who do you suppose'ld do a thing like that?
SYLVIA	Luckily, Greta had the sense the ring me first, so I was able to save her the trip.
FRANCES	It must be a bit of a surprise - finding us here.
SYLVIA	(to L. of FRANCES U.R.C.) In a way, yes. You see, I thought Max and Harry were having a regimental reunion.
MAX	A what?
SYLVIA	Perch said you were entertaining two old friends from the army.
MAX	I wonder what ever gave him that idea?
HELEN	After all, I wasn't even wearing my battledress.

A BIRD IN THE HAND

HARRY — Helen and Frances are old friends of ours.

FRANCES — We were all together in the trenches.

HELEN — Speak for yourself. I couldn't even get into a trench!

MAX — (embarrassed)   Well - how about another drink, girls?

SYLVIA — (down to R. of the sofa)   Oh, please don't let me interrupt the ballet class.

HARRY — No, it's quite all right, Sylvia - we're very glad to see you - honestly!

SYLVIA — You know, Harry, I think you really mean that.

HARRY — Believe me, I do!

SYLVIA — You really want me to stay?

HARRY — (smiling hopefully)   Yes, please!

SYLVIA — Well, we wouldn't dream of interrupting. Would we, Greta?

GRETA — Certainly not!

(SYLVIA and GRETA cross to the door R. MAX tries to stop them.)

MAX — You really don't have to go -

SYLVIA — If I'd known you were entertaining, I wouldn't have come over. But Greta said you told her you were going out to dinner, so I thought it was a good time to come and collect the rest of my things.

MAX — That's quite all right -

SYLVIA — I won't be very long -

MAX — There's no hurry -

SYLVIA — Then I'll get out of here - and leave you and Harry alone with the Tiller Girls.

(She and GRETA go out R. FRANCES moves down to L. of the armchair.)

FRANCES — And that is the lady you're getting rid of?

MAX — Er - yes - that's her!

FRANCES	(with a smile)	I think you're going to have your work cut out.

MAX Oh, no! It's all fixed - she's going! She just came back to get some things.

HELEN You seem to have a very civilised relationship.

MAX Yes. Well, we believe in that. No sense in not getting on together just because we don't get on together.

FRANCES I could never do that. If I'd seen my husband again - except in the divorce court - I'd probably have killed him. Wouldn't you, Helen?

HELEN Oh, no. I'd have thought about the money and held my punches.

MAX Oh, that isn't why Sylvia and I are being friendly about this -

HELEN Isn't it?

MAX No!

HELEN What is it, then?

MAX Well - it's - it's - well, we've been married twelve years! You can't hate each other after that!

(A pause. MAX has got slightly angry and has created a slight atmosphere. FRANCES breaks it.)

FRANCES Come on - let's put that music back on. (She starts to go towards the record player.)

HELEN Yes - this is supposed to be a party! (To HARRY.) Come on, Victor Sylvester - let's go!

(HARRY suddenly clutches at his stomach with an agonised cry. FRANCES stops R. of the sofa.)

HARRY Oooh!

MAX What's the matter?

HARRY Oh, my God!

HELEN What is it, Harry?

HARRY I got that pain again, Max.

A BIRD IN THE HAND

(MAX hastens to him, and assists him onto the sofa.)
(HARRY lies down. MAX sits beside him.)

FRANCES What's the matter with him?

MAX He has this bad duodenal trouble - hits him really hard. (To HARRY.) You lie right down. Get your head on this cushion.

HELEN (D.L. of the sofa) Has he had this often?

MAX Quite a few times -

FRANCES Won't it pass in a minute?

HARRY Ooooh! (Breathlessly.) No, Frances, this usually takes a little time. I - I have to rest - absolute peace and quiet - that's what the doctor said, wasn't it, Max?

MAX That's what he said all right.

HELEN Shouldn't he have it out?

HARRY Oooh!

MAX Oh, no - the doctor said he needs it.

HELEN Well, what is it?

MAX I dunno, but whatever it is he needs it.

FRANCES Maybe we'd better go, Max. What do you think?

(MAX looks at FRANCES and senses that she is aware of their subterfuge.)

MAX Well - if you girls wouldn't mind - it probably would be better.

FRANCES Okay. Come on, Helen. Let's get out of here.

(They go to collect their coats and bags, and return to R. of sofa.)

MAX Can you let yourselves out? I don't like to leave him when he's like this.

FRANCES Yes, sure.

HELEN You want us to call a doctor on the way?

MAX	(rising) No, that's all right - I'll phone him from here. He only lives around the corner.	
HELEN	So long then, Harry. We'll see you again - when you're feeling better. (She crosses to the door.)	
HARRY	(in pain) Yes, Helen - sure. Goodbye, girls. (He waves a feeble hand.)	
FRANCES	Be seeing you, Max.	
MAX	(a little embarrassed) Yes. You bet. We'll - we'll phone you - in a day or two, maybe.	
FRANCES	Fine. (She kisses him lightly on the cheek.) Only, Max -	
MAX	Yes?	
FRANCES	Try not to make it fifteen years this time. (She goes to join HELEN.)	
THE GIRLS	(together) So long!	
	(They go out, closing the door.)	
	(HARRY sits up, smiling broadly, and shakes hands with MAX. The door opens and FRANCES reappears. HARRY immediately lies down again with a cry of pain. MAX breaks away R. FRANCES smiles, picks up her carrier bag of shopping she brought in with her at the beginning of the scene.)	
FRANCES	Almost forgot my kipper fillets. Okay, Harry, you can relax now. We're going. (She smiles at MAX.) Goodbye, Max - (She goes out.)	
	(We hear the front door slam. HARRY sits up, relieved. MAX slumps onto the sofa next to HARRY, a bit subdued. There is quite a pause.)	
MAX	Whatever happened to them?	
HARRY	Nothing trivial, I can tell you that.	
MAX	Harry, you - (Pause.) - you don't suppose they were always like that, do you?	
HARRY	What are you talking about? They were a couple of dollies in the old days.	

MAX	Yes. That's what I thought. (Pause.) Do you suppose we seem like that - to other people? To those girls last night?
HARRY	You know, you're full of miserable questions, all of a sudden. (The eternal optimist.) Don't be silly, Max. How could we? I mean - well, we just couldn't! Men always improve with age. Everybody knows that.
MAX	(trying to cheer up) Yes. Yes, you're right.
HARRY	You're darn right I'm right. (He goes and pours a drink.)
	(A pause. MAX is still slightly subdued, thoughtful. HARRY chuckles.)
HARRY	H'm - Helen and Frances - that was really funny.
MAX	(turning to look at him) Funny? I thought it was sad. Those two poor women -
HARRY	(returning with the drinks) Poor women? They're loaded with alimony!
MAX	Maybe. But what have they got, Harry? I mean - what have they actually got? I tell you it's sad. They were pretty girls. Two pretty girls. And now look at them.
HARRY	So maybe they get comfort from their diamonds. Don't start feeling sorry for them, Max. They've had a good life.
MAX	Had, Harry? Had? They're not more than forty-five! What about from now on?
HARRY	What'll you bet they find themselves a couple of tired, rich business men? Oh, come on! Don't start getting melancholy. You know what you're like when you get melancholy.
MAX	You want to end up like them, Harry?
HARRY	I don't think those clothes would look good on me. You know, you should have kept off the drink. It always makes you miserable.
MAX	(sipping his drink, thoughtfully) What are we going to do?

HARRY   I can tell you what you're going to do.

MAX   What?

HARRY   You're going back to Sylvia.

(A pause. MAX looks up at HARRY for a second, then nods slowly.)

MAX   Yes.

HARRY   You see a couple of sad, lonely women and you go running straight back to your wife!

MAX   It wasn't that, Harry! Not just that, anyway.

(A pause.)

HARRY   No. No, I know it wasn't.

MAX   How do you know?

HARRY   You're still in love with Sylvia. Always have been.

MAX   Does it show as badly as that?

HARRY   (with a smile) It shows. So - you'd better tell her to start unpacking.

(They look at each other for a moment. MAX grins, sheepishly.)

MAX   Yes.

(SYLVIA comes in, carrying a suitcase and her handbag, ready to leave.)

SYLVIA   Oh - have the girls gone?

HARRY   Yes. Helen felt a bit sick.

SYLVIA   I thought she wasn't looking too good. Well - I'd better be on my way. (She starts to go.)

MAX   Oh, Sylvia - (He rises and intercepts her.)

SYLVIA   (stopping) Yes?

MAX   (magnanimously) You - er - you don't have to go.

SYLVIA   But, Max - we agreed.

MAX   I want you to stay.

A BIRD IN THE HAND

(She puts down the suitcase by the armchair and looks at him with a smile.)

SYLVIA
Tired of your bachelor life already?

MAX
Well, it's not that, Sylvia. But - er - Harry and I - we discussed the situation - and we decided that - well, I'm just not cut out for this - this other kind of life. Not any more. Oh, I tried! Harry knows I tried -

HARRY
Yes - he tried all right!

MAX
But it was no good, Sylvia. Whatever it was that I had, I haven't got it any more.

HARRY
Maybe you've got something else now.

MAX
Exactly! That's exactly what I mean! So - we decided - er - Harry and me - that maybe you and I ought to stay together. What do you say, Sylvia?

SYLVIA
Well, I have heard more charming proposals.

MAX
You know what I mean!

SYLVIA
Oh, yes. I know what you mean all right. And you expect me to say, 'If that's what you and Harry want, that's fine' ?

MAX
Well, damn it, he was out best man!

SYLVIA
It's not going to be that easy, Max. You're not going to cast me aside and then pick me up again when it suits you.

HARRY
(half-rising) Would you like me to go out of the room?

SYLVIA
You stay where you are, Harry Tyler!

(He subsides again, as she turns back to MAX.)

I'm not suddenly going to give up my magazine, y'know, just because you two come to a decision.

MAX
No. I know that, Sylvia. But you did say, didn't you, that you were going to do more work at home?

(SYLVIA gives a little smile.)

SYLVIA
Yes - I suppose I could do that -

MAX
Then I'd see more of you.

SYLVIA
Yes.

MAX	But on one condition.	
SYLVIA	And what's that?	
MAX	Miss Ferguson and her typewriter stay in the office!	
	(SYLVIA crosses below him to R. of the sofa.)	
SYLVIA	You and Harry have got everything worked out, haven't you?	
MAX	(pleased with himself) Well - that's all fixed, then!	
SYLVIA	No, it is not all fixed.	
MAX	What?	
SYLVIA	You're not going to get me back as easily as that.	
MAX	What do you mean?	
SYLVIA	If you want me, you're going to have to woo me all over again!	
MAX	I've been trying to tell you - I'm too old for wooing!	
SYLVIA	Well you should have thought of that before you invited those young girls here last night.	
MAX	But that wasn't -	
SYLVIA	You may be too old to woo them, buster - but you're not too old to woo me!	
HARRY	She's right, you know.	
MAX	Will you mind your own business?	
SYLVIA	Well - he was our best man!	
MAX	Look, Sylvia - darling - can't we talk about this?	
SYLVIA	No! (She stares back at him, defiantly.)	
	(MAX hesitates, glances at HARRY, hoping for assistance. HARRY smiles and shrugs.)	
MAX	All right - look - I tell you what I'll do. I'll - er - I'll take you out to eat!	
SYLVIA	Big deal! Ham sandwich and a cup of coffee?	
MAX	All right then. I'm going to take you to the smartest restaurant in town.	

A BIRD IN THE HAND 111

SYLVIA Oh, yes?

MAX We're going to have the greatest dinner you have ever eaten -

SYLVIA Oh, yes?

MAX I'm going to fill you full of wine -

SYLVIA Oh, yes?

MAX Then I'm going to bring you back here -

SYLVIA Oh, yes?

MAX And I am going to seduce you!

SYLVIA Now you're talking! Let's go.   (She takes his arm and makes a move to go.)

(MAX looks at HARRY, who rises and grins his approval.)

HARRY I - er - I'll move my things out by the time you get back.

MAX There's no hurry. Any time.

SYLVIA (to HARRY)   Are you coming along?

HARRY No, no. You kids go ahead. You don't want an old spinster like me around.

(SYLVIA moves down to HARRY.)

SYLVIA Harry, why don't you find yourself a nice girl -

HARRY And settle down!

SYLVIA Well, why not?

HARRY Too late, Sylvia. They only made one like you - and Max saw you first.

(She smiles.)

SYLVIA Same old Harry. Always got the guns firing.

HARRY You bet. Have a nice time.

SYLVIA (kissing him lightly on the cheek)   G'bye!   (She goes to the door.)

MAX So long, Harry. And thanks.

HARRY Be my guest!

112   A BIRD IN THE HAND   Act III

MAX   Oh - help yourself to your booze.

           (MAX and SYLVIA go out. The front door slams.)

           (HARRY, alone, surveys his drink bleakly and finishes it off. He has a thought, takes out his red address book and looks through it. He finds a name that appeals to him and dials the number, sitting on the sofa.)

HARRY   (into phone)   Hullo? Is that Patricia? This is Harry Tyler. Yes - well, I've been pretty busy. How about dinner tonight? You couldn't get what? A baby-sitter? Oh, I see. No, I didn't know that. Never mind, Patricia. Nice talking to you.

           (He hangs up dismally and crosses the name out of his book, then on an impulse throws the book into the wastepaper basket.)

           (GRETA FERGUSON comes in from R., with her coat on.)

           Going out, Miss Ferguson?

           (GRETA crosses to R. of the sofa, preparing to leave.)

GRETA   You don't suppose I'd stay in this flat alone with you? Thought I'd go to the pictures. There's an early Betty Grable at the Classic.

HARRY   Sounds great. Maybe get a pizza at that little Italian place on the way?

GRETA   I might.   (She goes to the steps.)

HARRY   (rising to R. of the sofa)   Any objection if I come along?

GRETA   (with a shrug)   Please yourself.

HARRY   (eagerly)   Just let me grab a tie.

GRETA   (unimpressed)   I'll call the lift.   (She goes out.)

HARRY   This is the first time I ever dated a daily lady!   (He goes out R.)

           (HARRY reappears at once with a tie and is putting it on in front of the looking-glass as MAX returns.)

A BIRD IN THE HAND

MAX — Sylvia forgot her handbag. (He picks it up from the armchair.) You going to stay in? Watch the telly?

HARRY — I am not! I have got myself a date. You remember Pat Shelley?

MAX — Er - no, I don't think so.

HARRY — (crossing to MAX) Oh, no, you wouldn't remember her. After your time. She is a real doll. Blonde hair, blue eyes - really great! I just phoned her. We're having dinner together.

MAX — Oh - fine.

HARRY — So - I may have to pick up my things in the morning - you know?

(They laugh.)

MAX — Have a good time.

HARRY — Thanks.

(MAX turns in the doorway.)

MAX — Oh, Harry - you won't be long, will you? Miss Ferguson is waiting at the lift. (He smiles and goes out.)

(HARRY reacts, collects his hat and starts to go. He stops in the doorway and turns. He looks at the flat, a little regretfully, then he has a thought and moves down to the wastepaper basket. He bends down and rescues his red address book. He looks at it for a second, shrugs as if to say, 'You never know' , puts it in his inside pocket and walks briskly out of the room.)

CURTAIN

FURNITURE & PROPERTY PLOT

ACT ONE

SET

U.R.	Padded window seat
U.C.	Leather armchair

U.L.	Bookshelves
	Recess
	  In it
	    Record player
	    L.P.'s
	  Cupboard

L.C.	Sofa
	Table
	  On it
	    Telephone
	    Cigarettes
	    Lighter
	Wastepaper basket

D.L.	Table
	  On it
	    Glasses
	    Drink including:
	      Whisky
	      Vodka
	      Gin
	      Brandy
	      Crème de Menthe
	      Beaujolais
	      Tonic
	      Tomato juice
	Tub chair

OFFSTAGE

U.L.	Two suitcases) Four parcels) Carrier bag containing) bottle of wine)	SYLVIA

U.L.	Typewriter)	GRETA	
	Handbag)		
	Crate of drinks including)		
	two bottles of whisky)	PERCH	
	Carrier bag of food)		
	Briefcase HARRY		

PERSONAL

	HARRY	Hat
		Watch
	SUE	Coat
	PEGGY	Coat

ACT TWO

OFFSTAGE

D.R.	Tray)		
	Suitcase)		
	Parcel)	SYLVIA	
	Small suitcase)		
	Coat)		
	Wedding photo in frame)	SUE	
	Coat)		
	Coat PEGGY		
	Hat HARRY		

PERSONAL

	SYLVIA	Apron
		Latchkey
	GRETA	Apron

INTERVAL

STRIKE all dirty glasses, ashtrays, etc. and generally tidy set.

ACT THREE

OFFSTAGE

U.L.	Briefcase)	
	In it)	HARRY
	Perfume spray)	
	Box of bottles including beer	PERCH
	Basket of shopping	GRETA
	Carrier bag of shopping	FRANCES
D.R.	Bathrobe)	MAX
	Glass of alka-seltzer)	
	Suitcase	SYLVIA
	Tie	HARRY

PERSONAL

HARRY	Hat
	Watch
	Red note book
	Money
PERCH	Cigarettes
	Change
GRETA	Handbag
	Coat
	Hat
HELEN	Handbag
	Coat
FRANCES	Handbag
	Coat
SYLVIA	Handbag

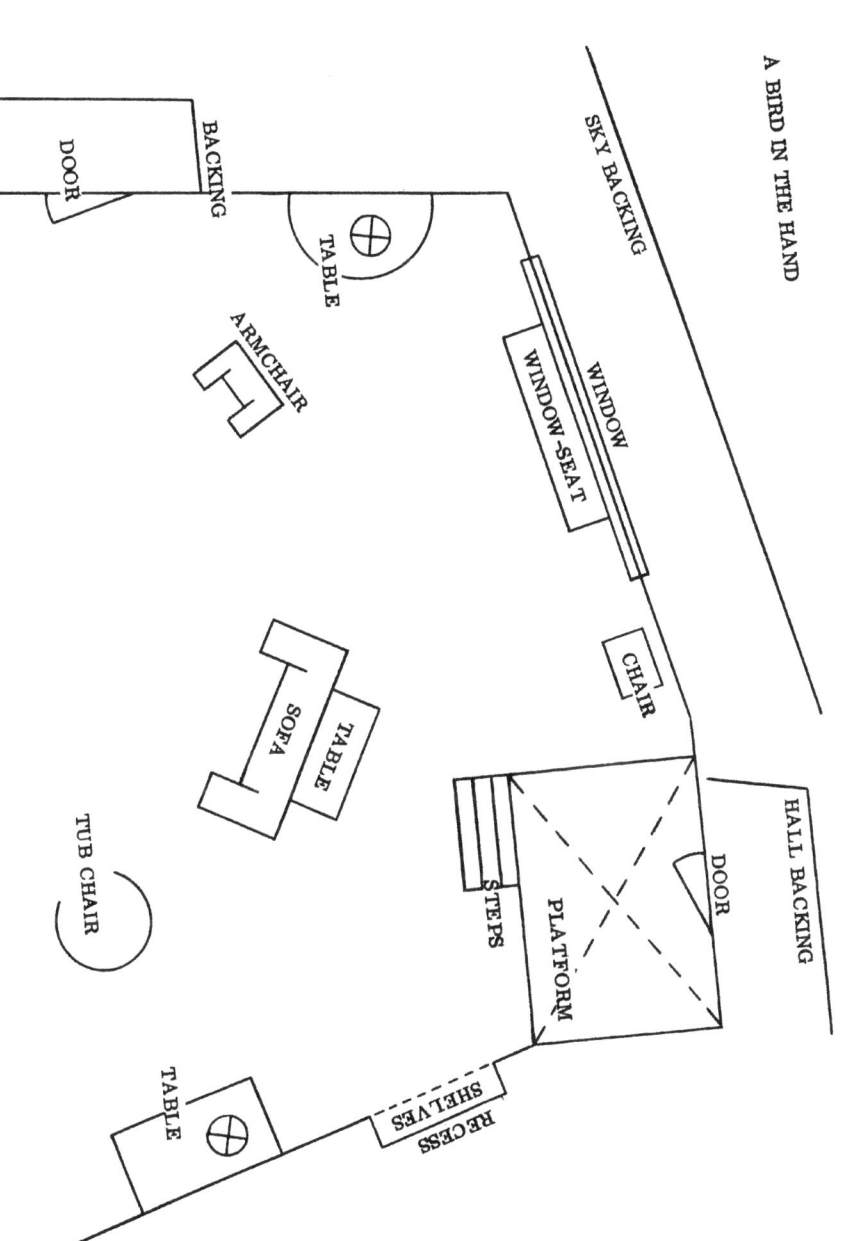

www.ingramcontent.com/pod-product-compliance
Ingram Content Group UK Ltd.
Pitfield, Milton Keynes, MK11 3LW, UK
UKHW021843210426
5322IPUK00022B/436